Husband, Wife, Father, Child, Master, Slave

Husband, Wife, Father, Child, Master, Slave

Peter through Roman Eyes

Kurt C. Schaefer

WIPF & STOCK · Eugene, Oregon

HUSBAND, WIFE, FATHER, CHILD, MASTER, SLAVE
Peter through Roman Eyes

Wipf & Stock
An Imprint of Wipf and Stock Publishers
199 W. 8th Ave., Suite 3
Eugene, OR 97401

www.wipfandstock.com

PAPERBACK ISBN: 978-1-5326-4063-6
HARDCOVER ISBN: 978-1-5326-4064-3
EBOOK ISBN: 978-1-5326-4065-0

Manufactured in the U.S.A.

John Mason, I miss you.

Contents

Acknowledgments

YOU WILL MEET ANNE on every page. Thirty-nine years of her resilience, good humor, concern for fairness, nose for weak logic, and love of a beautiful sentence have left their traces here.

My parents are here, too. With very little support they somehow crafted a marriage that puts Aristotle to shame.

Anne and I are in debt to Dr. Gayatri Devi and the lovely people of her New York Memory and Healthy Aging Services practice, where Anne worked while I took a leave of absence to write this book.

Along with Anne, these people read drafts and made helpful observations: W. James Bradley, Rachel Shafer and her family, Mary Hulst, Drew Kromminga, Wilbur Schaefer, Lois and Bob Nordling, Tracy Kuperus, and Stephen L. S. Smith.

I am particularly thankful to the New York Public Library's Stephen A. Schwarzman Building for taking me in as a researcher-in-residence. My work also heavily depended on the Manhattan Research Library Initiative, which granted generous access to the research holdings at Columbia University, Union Theological Seminary, and New York University.

I am also grateful for the cheerful, compassionate, competent work of organizations like Safe Haven Ministries in my hometown of Grand Rapids, Michigan. With grace and enthusiasm they actually form the sort of world that a book like this can only suggest.

I owe a great deal to my professors at Calvin Theological Seminary, who taught me to love and understand the languages and theology of the Bible, the elegance of its composition, and the brilliance of its authors.

The book's subtitle is a little homage to Kenneth Bailey, in whose tradition this book is gratefully offered.

And thank you to my history of economic thought seminar students at Calvin College, my SEO scholars at the Manhattan Leadership and Public Service High School, and my math scholars at Mustard Seed School in Hoboken, New Jersey! You helped me envision a book of serious scholarship that would also be enjoyable to read. Thank you for being my teachers.

Grand Rapids, Michigan
October 31, 2017

Husband, Wife, Father, Child, Master, Slave

ON TUESDAY, DECEMBER 20, 1859, *The New York Daily Tribune* re-ported extensively on the "Grand Union-Saving Meeting" of 7:00 p.m. the previous evening. The coverage sat there uncomfortably amidst articles on the aftermath of John Brown's October raid on Harper's Ferry, congressional debate on slavery and dissolution of the Union, and the upcoming 1860 Republican Party Convention. Monday's meeting at the 4,000-seat Academy of Music opera house, hub of elite urban social life, was crowded to standing-room. The gathering was led by Mayor Daniel F. Tiemann and former governor Washington Hunt. The Grand Union-Saving movement was dedicated to preserving the Union by maintaining the institutions of slavery.

New York City's prosperity was tied to the economics of slav-ery. In the years leading up to the American Revolution, about one-fourth of the city and environs' population was enslaved.[1] Before the official end of most slavery in New York (1827), Manhattan had been home to the highest proportion of slave-owning households outside of Charleston. Between 1820 and 1840, New York City's

---

1. Author's conservative calculations based on Foner, *Gateway to Freedom*, chapter 2.

exports grew from roughly equivalent to other large U.S. ports to larger than all other American ports combined, powered by slave-based cotton and tobacco trade.[2] New York City was also the major port of entry for cotton processed in Upstate textile mills. The banks of Manhattan held the promissory notes of plantation owners, who used this credit to buy seed and slaves, and used other slaves as collateral on the loans; some of the city's bankers also directly financed illegal slave trading. Thus an end to slavery would mean defaults on a large portion of the city's wealth. And the city had another slave-related export: Every summer 100,000 Southern plantation owners and their families escaped the miserable heat and humidity by taking extended stays in New York City. Tourism was a major source of revenue at a time when the city's population was only 500,000.

The ties and tradition surrounding slavery in New York City were so influential that on January 7, 1861, anticipating the imminent war, the city's mayor proposed to his aldermen that they should declare independence from the governments in Washington and Albany. New York City could become an independent, aristocratic city-state atop a network of slave-based estates—a facsimile of the political-economy Aristotle had proposed in his "household codes" twenty-two centuries earlier. Aristotle was adamant this was the natural and moral way to organize an economy.

But this was Christmas Week of 1859; 1861 was over a year away. Perhaps a war of secession could still be avoided. The Union-saving meeting began with a 132-gun salute accompanied by Roman candles. The stage banner quoted Daniel Webster: "I shall stand upon the Constitution. I need no other platform."[3]

The first two speakers were lawyer-politicians: James Brooks, Esq., and Charles O'Conor. Brooks, who edited the *New York Daily Express* from its founding in 1836 until his death, was between stints as a member of the U.S. House of Representatives. He would serve as a representative until he died in 1873, two months after

2. Glaeser, "Urban Colossus," 9–14.

3. "Grand Union-Saving Meeting." *The New York Daily Tribune*, December 20, 1859, 5.

being censured for attempted bribery. Brooks opined that those who invoke a "higher law" against slavery had

> broken up our Missionary stations, thrown discord into Tract Societies, and rent the Church of God in twain . . . When our Savior was on earth he was a subject of that vast slaveholding Roman Empire . . . and sixty millions of slaves, it is estimated, were in that empire. Judea, where he was from; Galilee, where he lived; Egypt, that he visited—all were slaveholding States . . . And now, if there be in the Holy Bible any such denunciations of Slavery or of slaveholders as we now daily hear from men calling themselves the servants of God, it is not in King James's . . . version of the Bible . . . But oh! Ye Scribes and Pharisees who rail at us publicans and sinners! . . . Ye Beechers and ye Cheevers, wiser and better than our Savior when on earth—go with your new version of the Bible into all the world, and shoos your Gospel into every living creature![4]

Charles O'Conor was then introduced. He had been the local U.S. District Attorney earlier in the decade. He would go on to become senior counsel to Jefferson Davis at his trial for treason, and eventually a nominee to challenge President Grant in the 1872 presidential election. Mr. O'Conor

> could not express the delight he felt in beholding . . . so vast an assembly. If anything could give assurance to those who doubted the permanence of our institutions and the support which the people of the North were prepared to give them, it was a meeting so large, respectable, and unanimous as this.[5]

The American Union, as presently constructed, was "time's last, most glorious, and beneficent production . . . We were created by an Omniscient Being, and in the benignity and the wisdom of His power"[6] he allowed mankind to gradually advance for 5,000

4. Ibid., 5.

5. Ibid., 5.

6. Ibid., 5

years before "He laid the foundations of a truly free, happy, and independent empire. [Applause.] Not until then was the earth mature for the laying of the foundations of this state."[7] The debate about slavery had mattered little

> as long as this discussion confined itself to societies with no more action than . . . the strong-minded women who believed that women were much better-qualified than men to perform the functions and offices usually performed by men. But, unfortunately, it had entered into the politics of the North.[8]

By precipitating secession, the North would break its covenant with the nation's founders, who had written slavery into the constitution.

Mr. O'Conor presented his case for slavery by contrast to Mr. Brooks. "If it could be maintained that negro slavery was unjust, then he would agree that there was a 'higher law' . . . But he believed that Slavery was just." Slavery is "benign in its influence on the white and on the black"; slavery is

> ordained by nature . . . a necessity created by nature itself . . . It carries with it duties for the black man, and duties for the white man, which duties cannot be performed except by the . . . perpetration of the system. [Cheers.] . . . As to the negro, . . . we denied to him every political right or the power to govern. Gentlemen, to that condition the negro is assigned by nature. [Bravo.] He has strength, and has the power to labor; but the hand which created him denied to him either the intellect to govern, or willingness to work . . . And that nature which deprived him of the will to labor, gave him a master to coerce that will . . . It is not injustice to leave the negro in the condition in which nature placed him . . . and the master to supply the government, in the control of which he is deficient; nor is it depriving him of any of his rights to compel him to labor in return.[9]

7. Ibid., 5
8. Ibid., 5.
9. Ibid., 5.

Was O'Conor aware his speech—both the comments about women, and the analysis of masters and slaves—paralleled Aristotle's household codes so closely that he might be accused of plagiarism? Prep-school-educated men of his day would certainly be familiar with Aristotle. John Wilkes Booth's undistinguished single year in a Southern boarding school (ages 12–13) included reading the classics; he could quote Brutus in Latin at the assassination and expect to be understood by his audience.

The Aristotle who just won't go away

The two lead speakers at that Unionist meeting give us a graphic portrayal of the themes at the heart of this book. Aristotle's household codes—his analysis of the proper economic and political roles of men, women, children, and slaves—served as the primary economics textbook in Western civilization for a millennium. Even when the classical empires declined, Aristotle's influence was perpetuated by a medieval fascination that included Thomas Aquinas's Aristotle-dependent *Summa Theologiae;* Aquinas argued in favor of slavery, subject to several conditions. Into the modern era, Aristotle held a prominent place in the curriculum of higher education. This was reinforced by the persistent influence of Aquinas's work, strengthened and codified by the 1879 encyclical *Aeterni Patris,* further buttressed by Pope Pius IX's 1866 affirmation that, subject to certain conditions, divine law does not forbid the purchase, sale, and exchange of slaves. As a matter of formal policy, this appears to have been the church's official position until the 1960s.

Like O'Conor, Aristotle presents the husband and master as having superior natural capacities—capacities that require obedience from spouse and slave. Like O'Conor, Aristotle presents this proper ordering of society as both an economic and moral issue. And for people like Brooks, Aristotle's analysis seemed to be repeated and authorized in the pages of the Bible—implicitly in the Old Testament and the life of Jesus, and explicitly in the New Testament's household codes that address the duties of husbands, wives, children, masters, and slaves in a form parallel to Aristotle's.

Aristotle's ideology did not die with the Civil War. Harvard's president emeritus, Charles William Eliot, warned the San Francisco Harvard Club in 1912[10] that racial purity was being undermined by the immigration of blacks, Irish Catholics, and Jews. "Each nation should keep its stock pure. There should be no blending of races." There should also be forced sterilization of the disabled, "moral defectives," and "criminalistics."

Eliot's remarks, articles, and conferences on race betterment drew no public criticism because they were utterly mainstream within Ivy League culture well into the twentieth century. President Woodrow Wilson famously praised the work of the KKK.[11] Eliot's successor (A. Lawrence Lowell, Harvard's president until 1933) argued for racial homogeneity, a quota on Jewish students at Harvard, and exclusion of blacks from living in Harvard's Yard. Many in the intellectual elite considered race betterment a progressive reform that would improve the world.

Some of the movement's energy went underground after the horrors of European fascism at mid-century. Yet even in our day desperate politicians find it expedient to scratch this deeply-felt itch for Aristotelian racism and sexism. Persons of faith are often among the first and loudest to shout their affirmation.

Perhaps it's been a while since you read some Aristotle, and perhaps the phrase "household code" seems off-putting. One

10. Quoted by Cohen, "Harvard's Eugenics Era," n.p.

11. For example, several quotes from Wilson's *A History of the American People* found their way into the film *The Birth of a Nation*. "The Policy of the congressional leaders wrought . . . a veritable overthrow of civilization in the South . . . in their determination to 'put the white South under the heel of the black South.'" (Wilson, *A History of the American People*, 50) "The white men of the South were aroused by the mere instinct of self-preservation to rid themselves, by fair means or foul, of the intolerable burden of governments sustained by the votes of ignorant negroes and conducted in the interest of adventurers . . . until at last there had sprung into existence a great Ku Klux Klan, a veritable empire of the South, to protect the Southern country." (This is the full book quotation that is summarized in the third screen quotation, ibid., 58). It is telling that, in recent discussions of Wilson's views, those who reject some criticisms as extreme do so, in part, by demonstrating how mainstream Wilson's opinions were. (For example, Scher, 2015).

friend told me it sounds "incredibly boring, like a list of rules that parents post for an uncooperative teenager." But he went on to say "you are in fact talking about something incredibly important and incredibly interesting," expectations for how we are to live in our most intimate relationships. That's exactly right. And these expectations shape not only domestic life, but the structure of the entire society, framing gender tensions, ethnic and racial practices and attitudes, and the fabric of political/economic opportunity and participation. These are fundamental issues that occupy much of our life as citizens, parents, partners, and co-workers. To live within our culture's practices while suffering from amnesia about their origins is to be at the mercy of powers that remain invisible and uncontrollable.

The shelf-life of a good economics textbook is usually about one generation if it is updated with a new edition every few years. Aristotle's economic analysis, by contrast, just won't go away, and it has become associated with the moral authority of large swaths of the Christian tradition. The book you are reading questions that association. We will approach the topic by going back to founding documents. We will emphasize the New Testament book of 1 Peter because of its extensive review of Aristotle's analysis, and because 1 Peter "is the only New Testament writing which systematically and thematically has addressed the issue of Christian alien residence within the structures of society."[12] What are we to make of the Bible's inclusion of household codes, which many have viewed as uncritical repetitions of Aristotle's analysis?

Current scholarship on the New Testament's household codes

In our day, there is relatively little scholarly literature that discusses the functions of these codes in the early Christian communities.[13]

12 Goppelt, *Der erste Petrusbrief*, 41.

13. Lincoln, "The Household Code and Wisdom Mode of Colossians," 93–112. In 1981, Elliott wrote that "A monograph or article directly on *oikos* in 1 Peter has yet to be written." (165)

Many—probably the large majority—of those scholars have something in common with James Brooks: They take the New Testament's discussions of husband, wife, parent, child, master, and slave to be, to a significant extent, an endorsement of Aristotle's positions. But they differ in the interpretation they give to this phenomenon. We will order these scholarly conversations by sorting them into three families of interpretation.

The end was near

Why might revolutionaries like Paul and Peter endorse the mainstream institutions of Aristotle's household code? Perhaps Paul and Peter expected the imminent—the *very* imminent—return of the Messiah, who would set everything right.

Imagine a band of French WWII resistance fighters in the very last days before they are liberated from fascism. Would their private communications be filled with ideological denunciations of Nazism? Probably not. You might instead expect them to be focused on surviving within the institutions that had been thrust upon them—making the best of a bad, fleeting situation.

This is one way of interpreting the New Testament's household codes, if one believes that they do little to challenge Aristotle. Consider Raymond E. Brown's *An Introduction to the New Testament,* which represents a centrist position within New Testament scholarship.[14] In discussing Paul's letter to Philemon, Brown observes that Paul thinks manumission—the release of slaves by their masters—is desirable:

---

14. I would also place Craddock (*First and Second Peter and Jude*) in this family of interpretation, arguing that the household codes represent an immature theology. For example, he explains the apparent endorsement of slavery thus: "Because the full impact of the gospel and its implications for social and political change had not yet been felt, 1 Peter 2:18–25 gives instructions for those in the church who are slaves . . . Let us not feel superior as though we came out of our baptism full grown and completely aware of all the freedoms we have been granted." 49, 51. By our Epilogue, I will be arguing that this interpretation has things almost exactly backward.

> Yet the fact that Paul, who thought that the end of the world was coming soon, did not condemn the social structure with its massive number of slaves was tragically misinterpreted for many centuries as Christian justification for the existence of slavery, indeed, of a slavery often harsher than existed in New Testament times.[15]

In discussing 1 Peter, Brown believes "there is no attention given here to changing the existing social and domestic order (even if it is unjust), but only how to behave in the present situation in a way that exemplifies the patience and self-giving of Christ."[16] The implication seems to be that the New Testament's authors *would have* objected to slavery, if they had thought the world as we know it was going to exist much longer.

Unfortunately, this explanation is at odds with most scholars' opinions about dating the New Testament's books. Like most others, Brown argues perhaps a half dozen of the letters attributed to Paul were indeed written by Paul, the earliest New Testament documents. But the gospels and the books containing the household codes—Ephesians, Colossians, and 1 Peter, with some related material in Titus and 1 Timothy—are all thought to have been written late in the first century (or even later), after the deaths of the apostles, as their followers realized Jesus' return *was not* imminent. That realization had an implication: the apostles' teaching and narratives must be committed to writing, and permanent church offices and practices must be institutionalized. If one accepts this thesis about authorship, it is difficult to simultaneously propose that Aristotle's codes were being adopted as minor accommodations in the face of imminent liberation.

Aristotle isn't so bad

Others have argued the New Testament authors endorsed versions of the Aristotelian codes that included personal kindliness toward

---

15. Brown, *An Introduction*, 68.
16. Ibid., 810.

slaves and women, while still intentionally mandating a patriarchal command-and-obey hierarchy over women and slaves.

There are two flavors of this option. One views this accommodation as virtually involuntary; slavery was essential to the Roman economy, and the early church would have self-destructed if it had resisted Imperial Rome's social conventions. Said more positively, a strong culture of households, as a political counter-weight to imperial power, created social space within which the church could flourish. Adopting and mandating the secular household code of conduct served evangelism, prevented libertine behavior, and could perhaps still be bent to conform with some notion of mutual respect. The various New Testament codes are taken to serve these purposes in varying degrees and by varying strategies, depending on the local circumstances to which they are written.

The two most influential studies of 1 Peter fall into this family. David L. Balch's landmark 1974 dissertation argued the author's purpose in 1 Peter

> is to reduce tension between society and church, to stop the slander. Christians must conform to the expectations of Hellenistic society, so that society will cease criticizing the new cult. The author of 1 Peter writes to advise the Christians who are being persecuted about how they may become socially-politically acceptable to their society.[17]

John H. Elliott responded[18] by arguing the motive of the epistle's author is not primarily about ending tension with outsiders; Elliott

17. Balch, *Let Wives*, 230. It will become clear enough why I reject this interpretation.

18. Elliott's analysis is unpersuasive for several reasons. In discussing 1:1's addressees, the "elect resident aliens (*parepidēmois*) of the diaspora," he rejects a metaphoric interpretation of "resident aliens" that would emphasize the recipients' alienation from a "heavenly home" (e.g., beginning at 129). He is correct in this, but in doing so he builds his entire interpretive framework upon an overly *literalistic* reading of "resident aliens." For Elliott, the recipients *must be* persons with the particular, official Roman legal status of *parepidēmois,* somewhere between "citizen" and "foreigner," "freedman" and "slave." (25) When pressed for support, he simply asserts that this *must be so.* (e.g., 131) He then uses modern sociological theories to speculate about how persons with such a legal status might have heard the message of 1 Peter; imitating Aristotle's

nonetheless argues, like Balch,[19] that Peter *does* endorse Aristotle's ideas as a way of creating a welcoming household-based church movement for social outcasts, a cohesive social order similar to, but with a distinct identity from, the surrounding culture:[20]

> Subordination to traditional figures of authority was appropriate in the household of faith. In the Christian perspective, to be sure, subordination and superordination are not prescriptions of the natural or social order; they are both social reflexes of faith in Jesus Christ and obedience to the Divine will which he demonstrated. Thus they are also appropriate expressions of *mutual* humility, care,

household would give such persons a social space to call "home," within which they could resist the many other ways in which they were pressured to conform to Roman standards. This interpretation of *parepidēmois* in 1:1 seems inconsistent with the matters later addressed in the letter. The adornments of wives of wealthy aristocrats, for example, and the role of wealthy household estates in the life of the church are topics that seem out of place if the letter is addressing those with the attenuated legal standing of literal *parepidēmois*; the letter also directly addresses slaves, who were beneath *parepidēmois* status. This is a general letter addressed to a diverse set of churches covering a region of 129,000 square miles; it seems heroic to think a single word in the introduction limits the message to one class of persons in those churches. The interpretation also seems inconsistent with the straightforward meanings we would expect the biblically-literate addressees to attach to the three forms of address in 1:1. All three were widely used in the Old Testament, and *parepidēmois* is used in the Septuagint as a designation for believers who are insulted for being zealous (Ps 69:8–9) yet must live in a socially tenuous situation (1 Chr 29:15; Ps 39:12, 119:19) while being accustomed to saddening hardships (Gen 23:4, 47:9). It is also a characteristic reference to God's people in the Babylonian captivity, mirrored in 1 Peter by the author's comment that he writes "from Babylon." Finally, LXX translates the Hebrew *ger* as either *paroikos*, related in meaning to *parepidēmois,* or as *proselytēs,* not clearly differentiating the two, leaving the word with a broad lexical range that can connote those who turn from belief in multiple gods, as did Abraham. (Fiorenza, *1 Peter*, 41). In the end, *parepidēmois* is a rich form of address that epitomizes the life of the entire church, as discussed in 1 Peter and the Hebrew Scriptures. Thus an interpretation of *parepidēmois* that is non-literal (not limited to those with a particular Roman legal status) yet non-Platonic (not invoking a "heavenly home," which several popular translations inappropriately insert into 1 Peter 1:1) seems in order.

19. Fiorenza, *1 Peter*, 45, for example.

20. Elliott, *A Home for the Homeless*, 190, 115.

and respect.[21] Such qualifications and modifications of interpersonal roles and relationships, however, proceed from and reflect the fact that "the patriarchal order of the household was indeed the social basis of primitive Christian life."[22]

This family of accommodationist views, common in academic circles,[23] faces a stiff headwind, since so much of the New Testament records Jesus' and the early church's joyful defiance of social conventions. The defiance seems particularly robust (as we shall see) when those conventions were built upon Aristotle's codes. And the accommodationist approach errs when it argues Roman slavery was helpful and essential to Rome's economic vitality, and thus "good for the slaves." By artificially depressing wages, slavery discouraged capital accumulation and innovation, the engines of productivity growth. This kept average incomes unnaturally depressed. Artificially low wages also prevented the emergence of a middle class with purchasing power, and thus fostered a relatively undiversified, slow-growth economy. For centuries after Augustus swept the pirates from the Mediterranean, the Empire was an

21. Here Elliott cites Kamlah, "Hypotassesthai," 241–43.

22. Ibid., 240.

23. Examples include MacDonald, *The Pauline Churches*; Judge, *The Social Pattern of Christian Groups in the First Century*, 75–76; the review by Gombis, "A Radically Different New Humanity"; Donelson, *I & II Peter and Jude*, 78; Keener, *Paul, Women and Wives*; Vinson et al., *1 & 2 Peter, Jude*, 120; Balch, *Let Wives be Submissive*; Elliott, *A Home for the Homeless*; Stagg, *New Testament Theology*; Crouch, *The Origin and Intention of the Colossian Haustafel*; Parsons, "Slavery and the New Testament"; Webb, *Slaves, Women and Homosexuals*; Witherington, *Letters and Homilies for Jewish Christians*, Volume II, 148; Cranfield, *The First Epistle of Peter*, 64; Best, *1 Peter*; Hills, *Common Life in the Early Church*; Krentz, "Order in the 'House' of God." Krentz offers a characteristic view: "When Peter urges house slaves to subject themselves to their masters, both good and harsh, he affirms the social structure of his day. He gives no hint that slaves might or should seek manumission as a goal, even though some scholars argue that manumission was an authentic possibility for slaves." (283; references Bradley, *Slavery and Society at Rome*, 162–65) For Krentz, 1 Peter "fits well into . . . ancient political theory . . . urges conduct that will make the nascent Christian community survive, even thrive, in the social structure of the time."

enormous trade zone under the rule of law; it should have become much more prosperous and resilient than it did. For the Empire's vast majority, slave or free, life was brutal, incomes were artificially depressed, and options were kept unnecessarily limited in order to promote dependence on the patronage of the elite. In Rome, as in the American South, slavery was only "good," if at all, for a tiny minority who were in power.

The other group, echoing James Brooks, argues the New Testament wisely adopted Aristotle's codes as deliberate normative teaching, ethically binding for all time. This view is not uncommon in American churches and, in my limited experience, on religious radio stations.[24] Wayne Grudem is a representative example—a prominent evangelical theologian, chair of biblical and systematic theology at a prominent evangelical seminary, co-founder of the Council on Biblical Manhood and Womanhood, general editor of the ESV Study Bible. His commentary on 1 Peter (in the Tyndale New Testament Commentaries series) takes the position[25] that Roman slavery was not so bad, roughly the equivalent of modern-day employment, and generally good for the slaves. Concerning gender, men must command and women must obey,[26] partly because women are weakened by their greater emotional sensitivity.[27] The analysis and conclusions closely parallel those of Aristotle.

As another example, Russ Dudrey[28], writing just after completing his PhD in Greek and Roman Classics at the University of Minnesota, argued Paul (and presumably Peter) had no moral obligation to attack injustices that we or they see in their world.[29] Aristotle's standards were so ubiquitous our instinct to think of the ancient world as repressive to slaves and women renders us

24. For example, Grudem, *The First Epistle of Peter*; Clowney, *The Message of 1 Peter*, 103–4. For a similar but pacifist rendering that draws on John Howard Yoder and Karl Barth, see Harink, *1 & 2 Peter*.

25. Grudem, *The First Epistle of Peter*, 124.

26. Ibid., 134–46.

27. Ibid., 144.

28. Dudrey, "'Submit Yourselves to One Another.'"

29. Ibid., 39.

"guilty of anachronistically retrojecting current social evaluations into (one's) reading of texts and understanding of social conditions that were very different in the world of the NT."[30] Paul is "a social realist rather than idealist."[31]

For Pastor Dudrey, who repeatedly identifies feminism as a major threat, the primary purpose of the New Testament codes is instead "to transform spiritually all who are in Christ . . . This in turn transforms all their relationships . . . We should pay renewed attention to the construct of mutual submission and reciprocal self-sacrifice that is the major force of the household codes."[32] The New Testament

> does teach the principle of the subordination of wives to husbands, of children to parents, of slaves to masters . . . We need still to uphold this principle as vital to the life of Christian society. Subordination to God-ordered authority undergirds Christian social ethics. This is not the foundation on which a tyrannical patriarchy rests: it is the nurturing environment for reciprocity within the legitimate structures of healthy families and a healthy society . . . The holy God calls us to obedience; Jesus calls us to deny ourselves and carry our crosses in loving self-sacrifice.[33]

I'm not sure this approach can quite support its own weight. For example, Pastor Dudrey goes on to argue the Ephesians code instructs husbands to not view their wives as possessions (after he argued that woman-as-possession was a universal belief in ancient cultures) and to love them and lay down their lives for them (whereas, he says, appeals to love or male self-sacrifice are rare in ancient discussions of marriage). Fathers, he argues, are told to not view children as possessions or be distant from them, but to have reciprocity (also extremely odd to ancient ears). And masters should *not* view slaves as possessions (though he argues ownership

30. Ibid., 40.
31. Ibid., 42.
32. Ibid., 40.
33. Ibid., 44.

of persons was, in this era, considered a self-evidently necessary arrangement), but instead masters should view themselves as fellow slaves (unthinkable for Aristotle!). "All of these Christian transformations of the perspective of those in power over the Roman household would have been earthshaking in the social world of the Roman *paterfamilias*."[34] Yes indeed! And they are all attacks on injustices in the social order, calls to costly political and social reform, denunciations of the reigning theoretical and ideological viewpoint of the surrounding culture. This would seem to undo the foundation for the author's initial thesis.

Besides failing to support its own weight, this line of reasoning (perhaps inadvertently?) openly speaks several shocking claims. Most authors in the genre will side-step the word slavery, morphing it into a polite "this passage means employees should be respectful." But that, of course, is not what the texts say. Employment did indeed exist in the ancient world, and was more common than slavery. These New Testament texts could have discussed the many moral issues that surround employment. They did not. They discuss slavery. Slavery is the ownership by some persons of other persons and their unborn offspring. Slavery is the coerced inability to direct one's own future, vocation, diet, sexual intimacy, location or relationships. Slavery is the arbitrary alienation of political, social, physical, and religious rights.

Mr. Dudrey makes no polite side-step of the issue: In this article, followers of Jesus are not obliged to raise objections to unjust practices, if those practices are common; the New Testament does indeed endorse slavery (and male super-ordination) as "God-ordained authority"; we should think of slavery not as tyrannical but as a principle "vital to the life of Christian society" and "Christian social ethics." In fact, slavery (and patriarchy) are part of a "nurturing environment" in a "healthy society;" both are matters essential for holiness, and the *apparent* attack on human dignity is actually an opportunity to "carry our crosses in loving self-sacrifice."[35]

34. Ibid., 40.
35. Ibid., 44.

The New Testament authors got it wrong

A different swath of New Testament scholarship argues the New Testament's household codes are insufficiently critical of the surrounding culture. These scholars generally accept the view that the codes were penned late in the first century (or later) and affirm Aristotle's codes. But they draw a different inference: If the earliest books, those closest to Jesus, are profoundly egalitarian (as in Galatians: "There is neither slave nor free, male nor female, . . . "), and the later books endorse slavery and patriarchy, this progression represents an unfortunate theological drift. Churches eventually settled into Roman imperial culture, and church leaders began to accommodate to their surroundings. The genuine, radical gospel was gradually eclipsed by an oppressive patriarchy, or worse yet, the entire New Testament presents an "unambiguously oppressive" ethic of patriarchy.[36] This view calls into question the message of the New Testament and the trajectory of the post-New Testament church.

Consider, for example,[37] the Oxford University Press's terse definition of household codes in the *Oxford Biblical Studies Online:*[38]

> The codes were an attempt by leaders of the Christian community to establish a pattern of family and social life not unlike that of traditional families among Gentile and Jewish contemporaries in the Graeco-Roman world. The patriarchal style represents a reaction against the egalitarian organization of the earliest Church in Jerusalem (Acts 2:44–7) and is remarkable for the absence of Paul's radical teaching against sexual discrimination (Gal 3:28).

36. For example, Standhartinger, "The Origin and Intention of the Household Code in the Letter to the Colossians"; Zamfir, *Men and Women in the Household of God,* 60–61; Corley, "1 Peter," 349–60; Fiorenza, *1 Peter,* 32.

37. Others include Elliot, *1 Peter,* who argues that 1 Peter presumes the inferiority of women (585).

38. http://www.oxfordbiblicalstudies.com/article/opr/t94/e912 Retrieved October 31, 2016.

Or consider the path-breaking and agenda-setting work of Elizabeth Schüssler Fiorenza,[39] who considers 1 Peter to be a document of imperialistic domination over a colonized, marginalized population:

> In any case, Asia Minor had been colonized for centuries and had absorbed Hellenistic language and culture as well as Roman imperial commerce and religion. This communication sent from the imperial center presents itself as an authoritative letter of advice and admonition to good conduct and subordination in the colonial public of the provinces.[40] . . . Thus, central to the rhetoric of the letter is the image of the household. Its inscribed argument engages the hegemonic socio-political and cultural discourses about household management (*peri oikonomias*) and about politics (*peri politeias*) which were inextricably intertwined in Greco-Roman political theory . . . We must ask whether the "meta-ideologizing" of some of the major contemporary interpretations of 1 Peter strengthens the colonizing rhetoric of the text by privileging its kyriarchal elements and by reading its egalitarian-decolonizing-dissent consciousness in terms of hegemonic consciousness that naturalizes kyriarchal power relations as "G*d's (*sic*) will".[41] . . . [H]*ypotassein* ("to subordinate") expresses a relation of ruling and power. Apocalyptic and cosmic language meta-mythologizes the kyriarchal order of the Empire . . . [T]he core of the letter . . . could be entitled: Become Colonial Subjects/ Subalterns. [42] . . . [I]t becomes obvious that the sender(s) the*logize(s) (*sic*) and moralize(s) the dominant kyriarchal ethos of Roman imperialism and request(s) that the subordinates realize and live it in their practices of subordination.[43] Contemporary exegetes are generally embarrassed by this rhetoric of subjection[44] . . . Biblical

39. See, e.g., Fiorenza, *1 Peter.*
40. Ibid., 23.
41. Ibid., 28.
42. Ibid., 31.
43. Ibid., 32.
44. Ibid., 33.

religions must cease to preach kyriarchal texts such as 1 Peter as the "word of G*d (*sic*)," since by doing so we continue to proclaim G*d (*sic*) as legitimating kyriarchal oppression.[45]

Fiorenza argues the task of the interpreter is to reconstruct, to "'hear into speech' the silenced voices, experiences and histories of the recipients to whom 1 Peter is addressed that are omitted or suppressed by the author(s),"[46] to "adopt a position that is not automatically on the author's side,"[47] since the author "demands their subordination to the kyriarchal colonizing powers of the Roman Empire against which movement of Jewish Messianism fought to defend their independent royal priestly peoplehood."[48]

An alternative

If I may summarize across all three strands of the current scholarship, there is a general agreement that the New Testament's household codes affirm Aristotle's analysis. The codes may counsel believers to pursue personal kindness within Roman social structures, but they do not offer an alternative to Aristotle.

My purpose in this book is to present a credible alternative to this consensus. Let me sketch the path I will take.

We will focus our attention on the household code in 1 Peter, the most fully-developed of the New Testament codes. It is Peter who first proclaims Jesus as Messiah, Peter who famously crumbles at Jesus' trial, Peter who is personally reinstated by Jesus, Peter who leads the church's tentative steps toward curious Gentiles. Whether penned literally by Peter, or by faithful colleagues expressing his teaching after his death, we would expect this first major encyclical from the chief apostle to be weighty and unencumbered by convention.

45. Ibid., 72.
46. Ibid., 51.
47. Ibid., 51.
48. Ibid., 45.

First Peter's centerpiece is its 27-verse household code, which closely tracks the topics in Aristotle's *Politics* household code—in Greek, the code for the *oikos*. Peter introduces his code with seven verses of direct preamble, which are in turn preceded by about 30 verses of general introduction. The household code is followed by several chapters that further develop the book's themes.

First Peter's introduction hammers away at principles and themes that are in direct opposition to those in Aristotle's preamble to his code. The verses that follow Peter's code draw out more teaching that is inconsistent with Aristotle, and refer to the church as the *oikos of God*; the church demonstrates its faithfulness by maintaining distinctive holiness and nonconformity in a hostile environment. Now I ask you: Is it at all likely that the first among the apostles would begin and end his book at odds with Aristotle, make the theme of his book resistance to dehumanizing Roman social norms, emphasize the equal status of all classes and blood lines under divine grace, and then interrupt his own logic to insert a code endorsing Aristotle? No, I don't think it is. Peter's code takes up the same topics as Aristotle's, and uses some of the same words and phrases Aristotle uses, but I will argue this is part of Peter's elegant way of disagreeing with Aristotle. Peter uses the *form* of a household code deliberately, to emphasize that the new identity of believers must find expression in new ways of behaving and treating others.

This book will carefully develop the basis for such a claim. We will begin by settling into Aristotle's way of thinking about the world in general and economics/politics in particular. Then we will trace the profound influence of these ideas and practices throughout the ancient Mediterranean, including the world of Jesus and the apostles. We will then enter into Peter's life and thought, which allows us to do a careful side-by-side reading of Aristotle's household code next to 1 Peter, the apostle's major letter to the churches.

2

Aristotle's World

To settle into the New Testament's household codes, we should first understand Aristotle. This is no small task.

Aristotle was the first person in the West, so far as we know, to set out an organizing system for all knowledge—to sort it into a comprehensive grid of topics, like biology, politics, ethics, physics, and personality. He then systematically organized a research project aimed at mastering all of those topics, *and* all of their interconnections. The scope and audacity of his project are stunning.

Unfortunately, only a small portion of his work has survived for us. Diogenes Laertius (c. 200–250 CE) still had access to much of the work that has since been lost, and estimated Aristotle had written 445,270 lines of text. By comparison, Homer's *Iliad* and *Odyssey*, the great Greek epic that predated Aristotle by several centuries and might have passed as the first comprehensive philosophic work, consist of just 27,800 lines. Homer is all in the form of heroic poetry, with no direct statements or analysis. The King James Bible is longer, but still only about one-fifth as voluminous as Aristotle's writings.

Though much of Aristotle's work has been lost, what survives still inspires respect. There are roughly thirty major works that span the breadth of human curiosity. Among these are complete works on dreams, sleep, and sleeplessness, the origins of animals, the progression of animals, the gait of animals, the parts of animals, the heavens, life and death, how it is that things come into and pass out of being, breathing, meteorology, physics, memory, sensation, the soul, virtue and vice, poetics, rhetoric, a brilliant and systematic treatment of logic, and—particularly of interest to us—two full volumes on ethics, economics, and politics.

As an example of Aristotle's method, consider his approach to the topic of constitutional politics. The events of his day generated interest in the relationship between the quality of everyday life and the political order—its constitutional makeup. Does good political order grow organically out of nature, or must it be projected onto nature, perhaps onto a nature that is hostile? Depending on how you answer that question, if there is a universally best form of government, what is it like? If you thought good order grows up easily from nature, this will be the constitution that best *conforms* to human nature and thus allows flourishing; if you think nature is hostile to good order, this will be the constitution that best *resists* the harmful elements of nature, and thereby allows flourishing. Whichever way you have been answering these questions, should you go on to imagine that good governance is like a *biological* entity, subject to a natural life cycle of growth and decay? Or is it more like a stable *physical property*?

Eventually we will explore some of Aristotle's answers to these questions. For now, consider *the way he went about developing those answers*. Characteristic of Aristotle's method and curiosity, he and his students set out to collate and compare hundreds of actual political constitutions as part of their research into these issues. Of this vast constitutional project, only a text of the Athenian Constitution has survived, but some of the project's results must surely be echoed in Aristotle's political treatises we will explore.

Aristotle lived in the fourth century (384–322) before the Christian era, a century twinned to the prior century by a story line worthy of Greek tragic theater. In this chapter we will place Aristotle in his cultural context by recounting the incredible events and ideas of those two centuries. Then we will become familiar with Aristotle's *Politics*, the volume that became the Mediterranean world's default economic/political textbook for centuries, and has influenced politics and economics in the West ever since.

Athens, 500–300 B.C.E.

It is a grim truth that the best orienting guideposts for our conversation will be two Greek wars. In each case we should think of war not as a continuous, all-consuming battle, but more like sporadic (though horrible), interconnected regional conflicts that gradually shifted power.

Our two guideposts:

1. Conflicts between the enormous Persian Empire and the many small, independent, Greek city-states ushered in the fifth century. From this emerged a victorious local Greek federation, led by Athens, and a diminished, but still enormous Persian empire which continued to exist, in one form or another, for a very long time.

2. Within a generation, the Athenian federation was challenged, and eventually humbled, by the Peloponnesian War (431–404) led by rival Greek city-state Sparta.

Thus we will be considering two centuries marked by warfare at their start and warfare near their middle. This is the world that shaped Aristotle's work.

Act One

Athens in 500 BCE was a small city-state—that is, an independent political entity, consisting of one city and a surrounding agricultural hinterland. Athens was by far the largest of the 1,500+ independent Greek city-states, but Athens still fielded a total population of only about 200,000. Many of these Athenians lived and farmed in the rural environs outside the city. About 35,000 of Athens's men qualified as citizens.

They faced an expanding Persian empire of approximately 49 million souls, roughly 45 percent of the entire world's population. In the preceding generation, the Persian emperor Cyrus had successfully expanded his holdings into Greek Ionia (modern western Turkey), Egypt, and some of the Greek islands. This same Cyrus is remembered with affection in the Hebrew Scriptures for having conquered Babylon and allowed the Jews to return to Jerusalem. For the Jews, Persian rule looked like a protected return to their homeland; for the Greeks, it meant domination and high taxes.

Despite their numbers, the Persian advance toward Greek lands was not without setbacks. There was even a formal Ionian revolt that was finally put down in 494 BCE. Now led by Darius, the Persians proceeded past Ionia, took Macedon (northeastern modern Greece), and set their sights on Athens. The Athenians would be made to pay for their support of the Ionian revolt.

The events of the next fifteen years left the world asking how it was possible that a tiny, consensus-driven, culture-oriented city-state could resist and defeat the world's undisputed superpower.

The answer seemed to be that when a culture pursues knowledge, rational discourse, orderly rhetoric, and consensual persuasion, all of which refined Athens's clever military preparation, that culture is able to do the impossible. Athens outthought and outmaneuvered Persia. Athens was prudent and courageous, whether in battle or in strategic retreat. Athens seemed to have mastered politics and economics. Athenians were well-organized, and made brilliantly maximal use of their limited resources.

Athens emerged as the unifying center of a federation of city-states. This federal system seemed to counterbalance the independence and fragility of the individual city-states—a structured equilibrium that Aristotle's *Politics* would seek to refine. High culture blossomed, epitomized by the reconstruction of the Athenian Acropolis. The ears of the world seemed tuned toward exploring Athenian ideas.

There were two broad avenues for this eager exploration: philosophy and drama. The first major wave of classical Greek philosophy, the so-called Sophists, began to study the relationships among political order, personal virtue, and quality of life. By raising questions, they developed a vocabulary for exploring answers. The dramatists, including Euripides, worked in the long Greek tradition of poetry and theater to indirectly explore similar issues. Some analysts point to this century as the origin of drama.

Two themes in the era's dramas will be particularly important for our work: fate and females. After Athens's stunning victories over Persia, it now seems entirely predictable that dramatists would ask: Are some things simply *fated*? We will see variations of this question echoing down the centuries. The fifth-century dramatists considered the fate, the assignment—the *moira* in Greek—of individuals, but also of *all* things. As the natural world has developed from chaos into an ordered, understandable whole, has each thing within that order developed properties, a nature— a *moira*? If so, when a thing does not remain within its assigned limits it may be trampling on something else's *moira*. That trampling process is a source of injustice and harm; it threatens to bring about a relapse toward the original chaos from which order has emerged. Therefore, the duty of each person—of each thing—is to pursue one's given capacities, one's *moira*, neither falling short of, nor exceeding one's natural boundaries. We shall see that this notion is central to Aristotle's politics and economics.

Is a human's *moira*—the allotted goal of a human person— related to that person's gender? Euripides and the Sophists created intellectual space for considering the role of women in culture. Before them "it would have been as superfluous to discuss seriously the role of women in marriage as to discuss the role of a domesticated dog or cat in the household."[1] Euripides considers unordered passion as a cause of turning from one's *moira*, and therefore a cause of injustice. He emphasizes the power of thought in restoring order and justice. And perhaps the tendencies toward thought or unordered passion are differently allocated across the sexes? If so, the sexes might have different roles to play in maintaining order and justice. These themes will also loom large in Aristotle's political/economic thought.

1. Arieti. *Philosophy and the Ancient World*, 147.

The pursuit of good order and justice—of understanding and maintaining them through analysis, reason, and contemplation—was the main project of the next century's philosophers. They had been primed to think that one's social standing and gender might affect one's role in maintaining that good order.

Act Two

If Athens was indeed fated to succeed against the Persians, it appears that this particular *moira* had a tragically short shelf life. In defeating the Persians, Athens accumulated disproportionate power and wealth from its small "empire" of formerly free city-states around the Aegean, and those newly-subservient locales quickly became restless. Athens overreached, attempting to invade Sicily, and failed miserably.

Envy within Athens's neighbor to the southwest—militarized, oligarchic, slave-powered Sparta—provided the igniting spark for the smoldering resentment within the Aegean federation. Athens went down to defeat in the Peloponnesian War, losing its naval power in the process. Only Sparta's clemency allowed Athens to escape the complete destruction and enslavement that was being demanded by Corinth and Thebes. Athens's brilliance was now subject to Sparta's war machine. In the process, total warfare had been pursued without rational restraint, economies had imploded and poverty had become widespread, democracy had lost its glamor, and regional civil wars had become common.

It is this context of turmoil, of dashed hopes and the need to reconstruct culture, that nurtured the three superlative Greek philosophers: Socrates, Plato, and Aristotle.

Socrates spends his humble life calmly, persistently asking the right (but uncomfortable) question at the right (but awkward) time. His questions fearlessly disrupt and reorient anyone who is going astray, particularly if they are going astray willfully or in arrogance. For this valuable but annoying service, Socrates was sentenced to death by the Athenians in 399 BCE.

We have no writings directly from Socrates. We know of his thought primarily from the dialogues penned by his student Plato (~428–348 BCE). If Socrates made a life of asking probing questions, Plato expanded upon that method, teaching through the medium of dialogues among casts of characters. These dialogues explore the questions that had been raised by the dramatists, the Sophists, and Socrates in the prior century. Strictly speaking, we do not know much about what Plato actually thought; his written work takes the form of conversations, in which the characters thought to represent Plato do not necessarily offer a consistent viewpoint. Perhaps this is actually Plato's legacy: The wit and beauty of the dialogues invite Plato's students into an orderly exploration of truth, rather than trying to nail down definitive answers.

Plato founded his Academy in Athens in about 387 BCE. A seventeen-year-old student arrived from central Macedonia in 367 and stayed for the next twenty years. He was not particularly popular with his teacher at first, because he openly disagreed with him and raised difficult questions of his own. This student was Aristotle. If Socrates and Plato invited their students into the pursuit of truth through reason, observation, and dialogue, Aristotle seems to have taken the bait—as if to say "All right, let's see how many questions we can answer if we give this method a lifetime of sustained effort."

Before summarizing Aristotle's work, particularly his *Politics,* we should consider a fourth great philosopher of this era, one whose practical effect on the shape of the world rivals that of our three superlatives. This is Isocrates (436–338 BCE), a contemporary of all three. His thought turned particularly toward the practical effect *in this world* of the virtues formed through philosophy and liberal education. He argued that under Athens's leadership a united Greek culture had the *duty* to conduct a culture war against the barbarians of Asia (read: The Persian Empire and its neighbors). Like Plato, he also established a school, and it was populated with the rising generation of Greek political leadership. Concerning the coming Greek culture war, led by Alexander the

Great of Macedonia, and discussed in our next chapter, Isocrates was prophetic.

Aristotle's Mentor

In his Socratic dialogue, *Republic,* c. 380, Aristotle's teacher, Plato, sets out the basic structure of his thinking about politics. He does this by considering the nature of justice, just persons, and just social orders. His logic is of a form we will encounter again: He first considers the nature of the human person, then builds outward from that internal order toward the nature of a proper political order.

Plato first observes a three-aspect human soul. We are simultaneously appetitive (we eat and have desires), spirited (we protect ourselves and have emotions), and rational (we think and weigh our options). In order to function properly, these three need to live in proper relationship to each other. In particular, if rationality (empowered by a proper education) does not lead appetite and spirit, problems will follow.

In the same way and by parallel logic, at the level of the *entire state* there must be three classes *of persons,* corresponding to the three elements of the human soul. Workers/producers are the appetitive, desiring, *epithymetikon* element, providing sustenance, producing and seeking pleasure, and often organizing their efforts around the medium of money. Guardians/warriors are the spirited, *thymoeides* element, acting to defend culture from internal and external threats. Rulers/philosopher-kings are the rational, deliberative, *logistikon* element. They should be stripped free of personal possessions so they may rule culture in an even-handed way, guided solely by their superior reason and education. Philosopher-kings are responsible to direct culture toward what is truly good.

Echoing earlier views concerning *moira,* each of the three elements of political culture must do its proper function, and not interfere in others' functions. In particular, the appetitive and spirited elements owe obedience to the rational, the element which properly rules. This arrangement is conducive to a just ordering of political culture. An unjust ordering of culture might, for example, have the spirited elements obey the appetitive. In our day we might point to the injustices that result when politicians (with spirited duties) become subservient to market forces or celebrity status (appetitive elements) rather than intelligent deliberation. That would be unjust because it demotes reason, the special capacity of humans, beneath the pursuit of pleasure and other appetites. This exiles humans to the province of beasts.

Plato's preferred arrangement of politics would also do away with marriage and nuclear families. Parents and children should not know each other. Anonymous breeding pairs should be eugenically selected by the philosopher-kings. This arrangement will create more personal freedom; as a result, individuals will pursue excellence by doing that which best conforms to their nature, and they will be rewarded only on the basis of merit. No more meddling parents or in-laws! No more nepotism!

For similar reasons, Plato's ideal has no slavery and no social distinctions between men and women. Universal liberal-arts education is provided, to encourage self-improvement for the common good.

Acknowledging that this political order is unlikely to emerge and persist, *The Republic* identifies four other, less desirable possibilities:

1. Timocracy—"honor-based" rule, where one's "honor" (*timos*) has usually been demonstrated by one's leadership in military conflict.

2. Oligarchy (or its cousin plutocracy)—rule by the few or the rich, who organize culture to serve their own financial interests.

3. Democracy (universal suffrage), which (says Plato) is inclined toward leadership by under-qualified demagogues who trumpet strongly-held minority opinions.

4. Tyranny (or "despotism")—rule by an unchecked, arbitrary personality.

The ordering of these four options is deliberate. If we can't be ruled by disinterested, unpropertied philosophers (literally "lovers of knowledge"), the best we can hope for is an experienced group of proven leaders that will maintain order over the appetitive class—a class that naturally grows over time. But this timocratic arrangement will tend to gradually devolve into an oligarchy/plutocracy; aristocrats will seek power, without demonstrating the honor that justifies this power. The excesses of these aristocrats become frustrating to the appetitive class, which makes up the majority of the population and eventually demands to receive leadership status as a group. This results in a crass and libertine democracy led by unqualified amateurs. Frustration with the unworkability of this system sows the seeds of despotism, in which a tyrant promises to restore order.

Inside Aristotle's Mind

Aristotle's thinking about political and economic order has some parallels with Plato's, but goes well beyond Plato in scope and detail. At the beginning of this chapter I said Aristotle set out an organizing grid for all knowledge, then analytically thought through the categories and their interconnections. Let's approach Aristotle's views on politics and economics by explaining his organizing grid for those topics. Then we can move on to his analysis of the items in the grid.

A theory of things: essence and telos

First, the very notion of categorizing *things* implies you have a theory about what counts as a particular *thing*—what makes something *this* sort of thing rather than *that* sort of thing. To do this, says Aristotle, you need to understand each thing's essence—you need to understand what each thing essentially is, what you might call its nature. Whereas Plato might direct our attention away from this actual thing to consider an idealized form of this thing, Aristotle directs us toward actually, carefully investigating this particular thing and its essence. And in order to understand a thing's essence you must understand its potentialities, its capacities—in Greek, its *telos,* what we might call its fully-actualized existence. You would not, for example, fully understand the essence of an acorn if you did not understand what an oak tree is.

Some of a thing's potentialities will exist by nature, and other potentialities may exist that are only achievable through effort. Most of an acorn's potentialities seem to be natural; healthy oak trees do exist that have not been tended by anyone. But humans are different. Some of your potentialities only bear fruit if they are nurtured. Though we might say someone is a natural at playing the piano, it actually takes a lot of focused effort and education to play the piano well. In and of itself a thing has only its *natural* potentialities. But a thing's *telos* is the condition of having all of its capacities, natural and acquired, fully actualized.

Once you understand a thing's *telos* you can begin to ask what its essence (that is, its nature) might be. *What is this thing?* What is it *in itself,* in virtue of itself, aside from any properties or accidents that might accompany it? What makes it *this* thing, and therefore different from *that other* thing? To continue our acorn-oak discussion, aside from being a tall oak tree or an oak tree in leaf or an oak tree that has just been blown over, what does it mean *to be an oak tree,* in all of these circumstances and incidental situations? How is that "oakiness" different from, for example "birchiness," or "bushiness?" These are questions about the thing's essence, its nature.

With those two notions to guide—*telos* (fully developed capacities) and essence (characteristic nature)—we could begin using them to think about humans, and eventually about human political/economic arrangements. *What is a human? What is the human telos? What is human nature/essence?* Aside from any accidental or circumstantial attributes some individuals might have, what does it mean *to be a human,* and not an oak tree or some other non-human?

Human essence and telos

For Aristotle, a human being is *an animal that reasons*. This is the essence of being a human; it is the human person's nature. To use Aristotle's phrasing, this is the combination of matter and form that is *human,* in its most unadulterated state. This is human nature.

At this point, since we are trying to put things into categories in order to analyze them, one might ask: Does this mean humans are entirely unlike the other things we encounter? Are there any commonalities among things? Aristotle's definition of human nature has already hinted there are commonalities between humans and other living things, because he has included the word "animal." Humans are *animals* that reason. On this issue Aristotle again departs from Plato. Aristotle argues all *living* things are a composition of two elements: body and soul. Body is in each case matter; soul is in each case the matter's form. These two are not separable; the *composition* of body and soul together expresses the nature and essence of each particular thing.

On the other hand, humans are really not the same thing— the same body and soul—as other animals. Humans are animals *that reason.* This distinction about human *nature* gives us a way to think about human *telos.*

The human soul has its own distinctive composition, consisting of three themes: intellect, sensation, and nutrition. (You might see Aristotle reworking Plato's reasoning/spirited/appetitive triangle here.) Each of these three is directed to some goal, some *telos,* some capacity to be developed. When they are developed properly, the earlier items in the list should direct the life of the later ones.

In your life, for example, you have a form (soul) that allows you to *reason*, while also allowing you to *sense* your surroundings, giving your reason some information about which to think. You simultaneously have signals that reach your senses and reason when you *need to eat* in order to continue sensing and reasoning. You are serving your overall *telos* when your intellect directs the response to sensation, and when sensation directs your pursuit of nutrition.

At times Aristotle's surviving writing simplifies his comments about human souls by saying they have just two themes: Intellect that must command, and sensation-plus-nutrition that must obey.

To summarize, we have thought through the nature and *telos* of human beings, hoping that this will help us understand how humans are different from other things. Our intention in all of this was to eventually understand how human economics and politics should be structured. If our conversation so far helps us think about what humans *are*—their *telos* and nature—we now need to think about what humans *do*. How shall we categorize the many practices, sciences, and disciplines humans pursue in accordance with their nature and *telos*, some of which constitute political and economic life?

Human action

Aristotle identifies three types of human activity: *productive* (making something that is actual, like making scalpels), *practical* (pursuing a practice or activity, like an apprenticeship in doing heart surgery), and *theoretical* (like studying how the heart functions—knowledge pursued for its own sake, though it may also have practical uses [for conducting heart surgery] or activity-related uses [for designing good scalpels]).

There is a hierarchy among these three sorts of activities. For Aristotle, theoretical activity is primary, a necessity if any of our practice and production are going to be done effectively. Theoretical activity is action that serves a universal, comprehensive, essential need, but production is not an obligatory activity. It is not a duty. This is because, unlike theoretical activity, it is not serving a universal need. It therefore is not serving the highest good (though it certainly does some good things). Production is also an activity that is not directed by a comprehensive plan for one's life. In this it is similar to child's play. It is not purposeful, not directed to a *telos,* and such unplanned activity is beneath reasoned consideration.

To be fully human one needs a plan and a *proper* plan, a life that is directed toward the right ultimate purposes.

We will come back to the details about highest good and right ultimate purposes very soon. For now, notice Aristotle's attitude toward productive activity leads to a low view of manual labor, and implies the "best" people are (and *should be*) exempt from doing it.

Having considered what humans *are* and what humans *do*, we may finally ask: What *should* humans do? If humans are, in the best case, reasoning animals whose intellect directs sensation and appetite, who are capable of producing, doing, and reasoning, could we be any more specific about what humans *should* think, produce, and do?

These questions drive the substance of Aristotle's *Nicomachean Ethics* and *Politics,* which we could think of as one extended discussion of just these issues. *Politics* is simply *Ethics* considered on a larger scale, as Aristotle indicates near the conclusion of *Ethics.* For him, politics and economics are both a part of a larger whole: moral theory.[2]

Aristotle is bold when identifying the things humans *should* do. An undirected, unplanned, unoriented life would not be worthy of analysis and is hardly worth living; a directed life should be directed to *the one right plan* that is appropriate for *every* human, the correct ultimate end, the worthy human *telos.* The words Aristotle uses for that end or purpose are usually translated "happiness" or "living well" or "the good life."

To most Americans this will probably sound like an endorsement of self-indulgence. Aristotle means something very different. The "*good*" in "the good life" indicates "desirable," following the best human desires, pursuing that life which is natural and common to all humans because it arises out of the best of human capacities and tendencies. The *good* life consists of activity aligned with excellences that are distinctive of rational human life. The good life—happiness—is a life of virtuous, wise, thoughtful

---

2. This attitude lived on until relatively recently. Adam Smith, after all, was a professor of moral philosophy. The first university positions in "economics" did not emerge in England until the eighteenth century.

character directed toward the common good of the community. The true goods in a human life satisfy good and natural human needs (which Aristotle distinguishes from mere wants). True needs cannot be bad for us, though education may be required for us to be aware of all of our true needs. If something is truly good for us, we should always desire it and we have a duty to pursue it. We *need* it, and it is impossible to have wrong needs.

Simply put, "the good life" consists of pursuing and getting all the things that are truly good to have—all that are genuinely good for us, our genuine needs. We pursue the good life by pursuing all our human capacities and tendencies in the right order and to the proper extent.

These goods would include the things necessary for physical survival, but humans are more than surviving animals. Therefore goods extend beyond necessities, to form an abundance that exceeds mere survival. And given that humans are rational and social by nature, the truly good life should include perpetual learning and active participation in the political order. This leads Aristotle to ask which form of human political/economic order is most conducive to achieving the good.

Human community

At this point you may be thinking "This all sounds fine. We are reasoning persons who should submit sensuality and appetite to thoughtfulness; we have a duty to achieve our potential and pursue happiness, properly defined. I like this kind of economic theory." But you would probably be quietly importing to Aristotle one of Plato's ideas: For Plato a human is a human is a human, and there are to be no social distinctions along the lines of gender or race or ethnicity or class or servitude. On these topics Aristotle now makes a shocking departure from his teacher.

Like Plato, Aristotle begins his consideration of economics by looking internally to the makeup of human persons, then looking outward to find a political order with parallel attributes.[3] We've already seen that when Aristotle looks inward he sees a soul that encompasses themes of both commanding and obeying. When he looks outward to politics and economics, he begins to see the same thing everywhere, beginning with the basic structure of Greek society, the order within the Greek city-state.

Aristotle argues the independent, freewheeling Greek household-estate, the *oikos*, the most basic building block of Greek culture, arises naturally out of meeting human needs. Thus the structure of the *oikos* is the most basic issue at stake in economics (*oikonomia*); the moral structure of the *oikos* is the fundamental moral imperative for the *oikonomia*. But this fundamentally appetitive/spirited *oikos* institution must be paired to a thoughtful, deliberative institution that will complement and direct the *oikos*. This pairing is a natural development of the *oikos's* need for social cohesion, an echo of the fact that humans are social creatures. For Aristotle, the spirited *oikos* finds its true place when it is part of a group of similar estates, bound together as a *polis*, a community of households rationally governing itself as a Greek city-state.

And when Aristotle gazes *into* those productive, spirited, extended-family *oikos* estates, he begins to see more and more cases that require a pairing between a dominant element and a dominated element—a reasoning element that must by nature rule, and a subservient element that must by nature obey. "The continuation of the human species requires two primitive forms of interpersonal relation, that between male and female for the purpose of reproduction and that between master and slave for survival."[4] And in each of these pairings (and by extension the pairing between father and children), Aristotle holds that the cooperative, egalitarian governance of the *polis* must be complemented in the *oikos* by a "total kingship" in which the patriarch controls all things. Marriages must consist of two parts: a rational, thinking (male) part that must command, and a sensual, appetitive

3. See, for example, Aristotle, *Politics*, I.5.
4. Ibid., I.2.

(female) part, weak in deliberative and rational faculties, that must obey. Across age boundaries Aristotle sees the same phenomenon: a male parent who must command, often distant and harsh, and a child who must obey.

The world of work likewise consists of two elements. The rational, educated, male head of household, the *oikogeneiarchis* (*paterfamilias* in Latin) who heads the *oikos,* must command. The slave, who from birth and by nature is utterly lacking in deliberative faculties, must obey. It would be *unnatural,* a transgression against *moira,* to have an economy without slavery, and it would be unnatural for slaves to attempt a life under their own command. For this reason, slaves are fit for the making sorts of human activities, but not the thinking, because making does not require a comprehensive life plan, but thinking does. If a person does not have liberty, there is no sense talking about a planned life, ordered toward some goals; "he who is by nature not his own but another's man, is by nature a slave."[5] This principle is loosely extended by Aristotle to all work, so that non-citizens, slaves, and resident aliens perform the necessary appetitive economic functions[6] while the aristocratic *polis*, with its superior rationality, directs the community.

Does this mean those who are by nature slaves are also by nature not truly or fully human? This would seem to be a clear implication of Aristotle's argument. On this issue Aristotle waffles. He sometimes suggests friendship might exist between master and slave, as the slave is "a part of the master, a living but separated part of his bodily frame . . . Where the relation of master and slave between them is natural they are friends and have a common interest" because what is good for the whole is good for the part.[7] But elsewhere Aristotle suggests the friendship may simply arise from the master's interest in preserving his financial investment.[8] After all, how could someone who lacks all deliberative capac-

5. Ibid., I.4.
6. Ibid., 1329a24–26.
7. Ibid., 1255b4–15.
8. Ibid., 1278b32–37.

ity perceive he has a common interest with the master—that the master's well-being affects his own—and thus be a friend? So in *Ethics,* Aristotle asserts there could be no friendship where there is nothing in common—craftsman and tools, farmer and draft animals, master and slave. On the other hand, he indicates slaves are different from lower animals because slaves can apprehend others' reasoned analysis, though they are not capable of doing such analysis for themselves.[9] *And yet,* in the same paragraph Aristotle says the difference between master and slave is akin to the difference between human and beast; "indeed the use made of slaves and of tame animals is not very different."

In the end it is probably fair to say Aristotle portrays natural slaves as diminished humans, who are doing what is best for themselves when they submit to the rational direction of their masters.

Seriously?!

Aristotle knew some slaves in Greece had become chattel as a result of being on the wrong side of a military action. They had led prosperous, fulfilling, self-directed lives before enslavement, and Aristotle grants that in such cases of "slavery by law rather than by nature" the slave may be fit for more than servitude and domination. But he is not consistent in working out the implications of this observation. And by what principle are all other slaves, by birth or poverty or simple bad luck, identified as sub-human? Surely Aristotle had deeply engaged the egalitarian ideas of his teacher Plato. Where is Aristotle's reasoned, measured engagement with those ideas? When they briefly surface as Socrates' opinions,[10] Aristotle simply asserts without analysis that they are incorrect.

> Aristotle fails to provide a justification of slavery as actually practiced either in the Greek world or in any other known society . . . he gives no reason to believe that there are any natural slaves . . . The very idea of a *community*

9. Ibid., I.5.
10. Ibid., I.8.

> of natural slaves is incoherent; yet . . . [h]e envisages that
> barbarian peoples are just such communities, adapted
> by nature to serve as a continual source of slaves for the
> Greeks (1252b7–9)[11]

Some might excuse Aristotle with a breezy "well, that's just the way people thought back then," but surely that wouldn't explain anything. We have seen that Plato *most assuredly did not think in this way,* and Aristotle has willfully thrown off Plato on these topics. Furthermore, Aristotle made a life of going against the received wisdom in dozens of ways, such that he eventually had to flee Athens. This is not the sort of person who thoughtlessly goes along with the crowd.

Some scholars argue, on the basis of several gaffes and inconsistencies within *Politics,* that the manuscript may have been Aristotle's lecture notes for classes at his academy; perhaps he would have nuanced, explained, and smoothed rough edges extemporaneously during the lecture. In fact, some have argued *none* of the documents Aristotle wrote for publication have survived, and we only have lecture notes and other informal documents, but as an explanation for Aristotle's attitude toward slavery, this seems unlikely. Whether as lecture notes or a formal treatise, the manuscript is addressed to the *oikogeneiarchis / paterfamilias,* and there does not appear to be a way of resolving the "gaffes" without eliminating much of the basic analytical structure of the book.

The fact is we do not know what Aristotle's motives were, but we do know that *Politics,* as written, was received as the most influential of the classical Greek documents on political order, having a substantial effect on Western culture for centuries. In fact, if you are familiar with the American founding, you may recognize its influence there as well. *The Declaration of Independence* asserts a duty to engage three natural goods: life, liberty, and pursuit of happiness. This appears to come from Aristotle's ethical theory. Like Plato and Aristotle, the founders were suspicious of universal-franchise democracy, and thus wrote a Constitution in which voting rights were restricted to the aristocracy—free male

11. Taylor, *Politics,* 257.

landholders—with the Senate and President not directly elected by even these aristocratic voters. The founders spoke boldly of all men being created equal, even while many owned slaves. For a justification of chattel human slavery, they needed to look no further than Aristotle's *Politics*.

3

Alexander and the
Culture-War Empire

I HAVE BEEN WORKING on this book for nearly a decade. If a friend asked "What are you up to?" I might say something brave, like "I think in 1 Peter the Apostle gave us a point-by-point analysis of Aristotle's household codes." Very soon thereafter I usually heard something like this: "But wasn't Peter just really stupid?" Weren't the disciples illiterate peasants from a backwater region of an insignificant country? How would they know about Aristotle, much less write a critique of his ideas?

If we put the logic behind those questions into a classic Greek syllogism, it could look like this:

1. None of the working-class people I know has ever heard of Aristotle's household codes.

2. Jesus' disciples were working-class people.

3. Therefore, Jesus' disciples didn't know about Aristotle's household codes.

You can see that, even if statements 1 and 2 were true, statement 3 makes several leaps that haven't been justified.

A better syllogism would look like this:

1. Every working-class American immediately knows what I'm talking about if I say "four score and seven years ago," "a date that will live in infamy," or "life, liberty, and the pursuit of happiness." They intuitively see what's happening if someone misquotes such a phrase—say, an advertisement that speaks of "life, liberty, and the pursuit of chocolate."

2. In first-century Palestine, Aristotle's household codes were a familiar part of the cultural landscape, in the same way these twenty-first-century American phrases are today.

3. Therefore, the early Christian disciples and those around them very likely understood what Aristotle's household codes were and what they required. And if the codes were wryly misquoted for effect, people would generally understand, and appreciate the humor.

How did classical Greek ideas and culture become so familiar in first-century Palestine? This chapter tells the story.

Alexander's Culture War

We have seen that fourth-century-BCE Greece liked the suggestion of bringing excellence to the Eastern empires by conquering them, then infusing them with Greek culture and philosophy. At the same time this notion became popular, Aristotle was systematizing and codifying Greek culture and philosophy. These two social movements came together in the person of Alexander III the Great of Macedonia.

Alexander's father, Philip II, set the stage by honing Macedonia's military might and employing Aristotle as Alexander's personal tutor. Alexander would be given both the military means and the intellectual capacity to fulfill the Greek dream: a world politically united and culturally renewed, a world in which reason and discourse would displace the (in their opinion) hysterical, superstitious, blood-soaked Eastern religions, a world where civility and prosperity could emerge and mature. And the venture would not be a bad deal for Alexander and Macedonia, either.

In weighing potential tutors for his thirteen-year-old son, Philip considered Isocrates, the fountainhead of the Greek cultural war motif. Isocrates was already the tutor of many other aspiring Greek leaders. Perhaps Philip rejected Isocrates because Philip thought he himself could do an adequate job of instilling the imperial vision within Alexander. In the end Philip chose Aristotle, and set up the apprenticeship in Mieza's Temple of the Nymphs. This venture also became the school of other young nobility. They eventually became some of Alexander's friends, generals, and, in some cases, successors.

Philip II's thirty-three-year reign began in a Macedonia that was a small state in the shadows of its neighbors to the southwest— Athens, Sparta, and Thebes. He led Macedonia to dominance over the entire Greek civilization. His military innovations—heavily armored cavalry, light infantry organized into responsive phalanxes rather than mob lines of battle, and lengthened spears that exceeded the thrust of the opposition—subdued the historically stronger Greek states. This led to Philip II's election as the commander of an invasion of the Persian Empire.

With the invasion just beginning, Philip II was assassinated in 336 BCE and was succeeded by his twenty-year-old son, Alexander III. The motives for the assassination by his chief bodyguard are obscure, though Alexander's mother seems to have been unrestrained in her praise of the assassin. She and Alexander then turned to the unpleasant work of assassinating six potential heirs to Philip's throne. They then had to put down multiple new Greek revolts on two fronts, all inspired by Philip's demise.

Having restored relative order at home, Alexander turned eastward. Philip might have been content to punish the Persians by conquering the Greek-influenced parts of Asia Minor, but Alexander's initial blitzkrieg success there seems to have confirmed his vision of what was possible among the eastern "barbarians." After taking Asia Minor—the Persian emperor Darius III fled at Issus, leaving behind his wife, mother, and two daughters who had to be ransomed—Alexander turned south. He subdued Syria and Palestine by besieging Tyre and then Gaza. In each case he massacred the men of military age and sold their children and wives into slavery. Alexander leveled Tyre and, like the Persians before him and the Romans after him, he made Samaria his base of operations in Palestine. Samaritans were local insiders who also hated Jewish rule, and they were a minor political force that was easily made codependent.

The Jews, on the other hand, were substantial. We have no reliable population estimates from this era, but Jews were probably around 7 percent of the population of the (later) Roman Empire. They thus required active management by any aspiring empire. Though the animosity between Jews and Samaritans was not new, the Samaritans' role as toadies under successive conquering empires made things worse. Samaritans were a daily reminder to Jews of the pagans' culture wars that were directed, in part, against Jews.

Alexander marched on from Palestine to Egypt, where he was received as a liberator. An oracle declared him The Son of God (Amun/Ammon, an approximate cultural equivalent of Zeus). Then Alexander turned back to the northeast to attack the Persian homeland, conquering the Persian/Achaemenid Empire in its entirety. Hoping to dominate the world all the way to the unknown Great Outer Sea, Alexander invaded India, where he encountered attack elephants for the first time. His battle-weary soldiers eventually prevailed upon him to return to Babylon, which he envisioned as the new imperial seat, to consolidate his holdings. There he died, a few weeks short of his thirty-third birthday.

Between 334 and 323 BCE, Alexander had created a unified Greek world empire and cultural colossus, stretching from Greece to India. It was punctuated by twenty new colonial-city cultural-centers that bore his name (Alexandria), missionary centers for the dispersion of Greek culture. Their schools, theater performances incorporating cult ceremonies, governmental institutions, currency, language, businesses, and gymnasiums—centers of learning, debate, and culture, as well as exercise and competition—promoted Greek cultural dominance throughout the immense empire. This cultural dominance endured in the eastern Mediterranean even after Rome defeated the Greek empire's last vestigial rulers,

Cleopatra and Mark Antony, in 31 BCE. A comprehensive culture that was fundamentally Greek was not displaced until the coming of Islam in the seventh century CE. The Hellenistic Age—from *hellén*, Greek for "a Greek"—had begun.

Life after Alexander

Alexander died suddenly with no apparent heir. There followed 40 years of warfare among the *Diadochi* ("successors"), former generals and friends now jostling for power.

Alexander's empire eventually fractured into four parts. Egypt and southern Palestine, including Judea, went to Ptolemy, one of Alexander's generals and a former fellow student under Aristotle. Ptolemy ruled from Egypt's Alexandria. The Macedonian homeland went to the dynasty of Antigonus, another of Alexander's generals. Western Asia Minor was eventually led by the Attalid dynasty after the death of Lysimachus, yet another of Alexander's generals.

Everything else—the geographic majority of Alexander's empire, everything from Syria east to India—became the Seleucid Empire. It was led from Seleucia on the Tigris, with a secondary capital at Syrian Antioch on the Orontes River, near the northeast corner of the Mediterranean Sea. The Seleucid Empire was initially led by Seleucus I Nicator ("Seleucus the Conqueror"), an infantry general under Alexander. Following Alexander's death, Seleucus had participated in the conspiracy to assassinate the empire's regent. After seizing power, Seleucus had to ruthlessly reconquer much of the vast territory of his empire.

This fracturing of Alexander's lands placed Palestine awkwardly on the border between two Greek empires—the Seleucid and the Ptolemaic. During Judea's initial 120 years in the Ptolemaic Empire, the Jews were considered a small, pacified temple-state led by its priestly class—essentially a religious city-state. So long as they paid their taxes, they were often allowed substantial liberties.

But not all Jews lived in Judea. They had already been dispersed by famine, warfare, captivities, and voluntary migration.

Jewish migration among the empires' cities continued to be routine, with a sizable Jewish community (in fact, probably the largest Jewish community anywhere) in cultured (Egyptian, Ptolemaic) Alexandria. Population estimates around the turn of the millennium will again give a sense of the geographic dispersion of Jews: Perhaps a million Jews in Egypt (Alexandria's half-million inhabitants were 40 percent Jewish), perhaps 700,000 in Judea, perhaps another million in (Seleucid) Lebanon/Syria, and perhaps a million or more scattered elsewhere. Though the sum of these numbers is open to debate, the extent of their geographic distribution is not. By the turn of the millennium more Jews spoke Greek than Hebrew.

Jews who were dispersed throughout the Hellenistic empires (the Jewish diaspora) participated in festival gatherings in Jerusalem three times each year. We have reason to believe this in-gathering was substantial. Though the population of all Judea was likely around 700,000 in the first century CE, Josephus records that when Jerusalem was besieged and fell *at Passover* in 70 CE, 1,100,000 were killed and an additional 97,000 were sold as slaves. As Jews across the Greek empires faced the pressures of Hellenization, their pilgrimage rituals assured that the entire community was informed of each region's experiences.

Acculturation to Hellenism was gradual but persistent, often feared by the priests yet undeniably widespread. Its symptoms ranged from changes in clothing styles to the practice of male reverse-circumcision. (How could a man participate in Greek gymnasium culture, which epitomized and virtually idolized the rational control of physical perfection, if his body bears the shame of ritual mutilation?)

The assimilation to Hellenism was already substantial enough by the middle of the third century BCE—within just one lifespan of the start of the Ptolemaic Empire—that Egypt's Alexandrian Jews translated the Torah into *koine* Greek. Jews were adopting the common language and losing fluency in Hebrew. The rest of the Hebrew Scriptures, and additional Hebrew sacred writings, were translated into Greek within roughly a century, becoming the

Septuagint (usually noted as LXX) by mid-second century BCE. This Septuagint is the default version of the Scriptures for Jews living outside of Palestine, Jews who may have read little Hebrew; it is the version usually quoted by Paul in the New Testament. The New Testament certainly seems to present both Paul and Jesus as moving easily among conversations in Aramaic (among Galileans, for example), Hebrew (in synagogues and temple), and Greek (for example, during Jesus' side-trip to Syrophoenicia), and perhaps also Latin (with centurions, and with Roman officialdom at trials). Of the roughly 1,600 *Jewish* funeral inscriptions that have been found in Palestine dated between 300 BCE and 500 CE, about 70 percent are in Greek, 12 percent in Latin, and only 18 percent in Hebrew or Aramaic.[1]

Leaning against the forces of assimilation, the sacred writings in Hebrew probably formed the core curriculum for Jewish boys' primary education, at least in Palestine. Retaining the Hebrew language and its sacred writings cut in two directions: it resisted assimilation to Greek culture and ideas, the *lingua franca* to Palestine's west, and it simultaneously resisted syncretism with the culture and ancient ideas associated with Aramaic, the *lingua franca* of the lands to the east. Aramaic had been an everyday, native language of many Palestinian Jews since the Babylonian captivity (sixth century BCE). Hebrew school helped Jews maintain some cultural integrity and distinctiveness, and it was not a great leap for Aramaic-speaking boys to study Hebrew: the difference has been likened to Portuguese boys learning Spanish (two languages in the same family, sharing the same script), or Danes learning Swedish.

There is much that is not known about schooling in Palestine in this era—there are descriptions from several centuries later, and scholars disagree in their willingness to consider them applicable to earlier times. But it seems probable that instruction in Hebrew began for boys around the age of 5 and continued in some form until puberty. Jesus' facility in debating the Scriptures in Jerusalem's temple, even at an early age, and his ability to spontaneously read from Hebrew scrolls during worship, certainly suggest he had

1. Van Der Horst, "Jewish Funerary Inscriptions," 48.

formal education in reading Hebrew, along with extended discussions of the Scriptures in the setting of a synagogue.

In some eras, a few boys probably continued schooling beyond puberty for an advanced education under the direction of a tutor or Rabbi. Although in later eras a tradition of bachelorhood developed within Judaism, in the first century BCE, boys were probably expected to marry, and most probably did so while in their late teens. (We know of curses, dating from a bit after the first century, upon those not married by the age of 20, along with prohibitions on marriage before 13.) Hebrew school was probably conducted in the mornings, followed in the afternoon by an apprenticeship to some trade or craft.

The Hebrew texts that were the core of this education fall into three categories: the Law, the Prophets, and the writings.[2] By soon after the return from exile there was consensus concerning which documents were considered authoritative Torah. Consensus regarding the authoritative prophets was reached by the end of the second century BCE, around the time of the completion of the Septuagint. But the definitive judgment concerning which "writings" should be considered authoritative was not concluded until a bit after Jesus' time, several centuries after the formation of the Septuagint. (The surviving early Septuagint manuscripts differ in the books they include.)

In the end, roughly ten books of the Septuagint were not included in the eventual Hebrew canon of writings. (They are therefore also excluded from Protestant editions of the sacred Scriptures). This is important for us because these ten books *were* widely in use among Jews in the first century CE, and some of them show familiarity with Greek philosophical ideas (e.g., *Wisdom)* and/or were composed in Greek (*Wisdom, II Maccabees*). They provide one more piece of evidence that knowledge of Greek philosophical categories was likely widespread among Jews in the New Testament period.

---

2. Hence the name for the sacred Scriptures: *Tanakh*, from Torah/law, Nevi'im/prophets, and Ketuvim/writings.

We also know that teaching about the household codes, particularly their attitudes toward women, finds its way into rabbinic teachings of the last centuries BCE. One notable instance is the work of the influential Yesha Ben Sira, teaching early in the second century BCE, the source of the Septuagint's Book of Sirach/Ecclesiasticus. Whereas the earliest extant Jewish wedding contract (around 500 BCE, before Greek influence) gives a detailed account of a surprisingly egalitarian marriage (she has her own property, can dispense with it as she wishes, has divorce rights equal to her husband's), three centuries later Ben Sira sometimes displays a shockingly negative attitude toward women.[3] His writing coincided with the transition from Ptolemaic control of Judea, to which we now turn.

The Seleucid Captivity

Around the beginning of the second century BCE, the Seleucid emperor Antiochus III, beset on the other frontiers of his empire, turned south and waged war on the Ptolemaic Empire. He took Judea and conquered Egypt as far as Alexandria, but his success was short-lived; Rome was slowly emerging from the west as the new imperial superpower. Forced to confront Rome at the Battle of Magnesia in 189 BCE, Antiochus lost 53,000 men, while Rome suffered a mere 400 casualties. Antiochus II, exercising a strategy that is becoming familiar by now, fled the battle. In the resulting lopsided peace, he lost Egypt, his war elephants, and his fleet. Judea stood as his only enduring conquest. Asia Minor was now a tributary of Rome, the Seleucid Empire was imploding, and Rome had imposed crushing war indemnity payments on the Seleucids.

---

3. For example, the conclusion of his discourse on daughters (Sir 42:14–16) reads "Better the wickedness of a man than the goodness of a woman." He generalizes about the headstrong daughter thus: "She will sit in front of every tent peg and open her quiver to every arrow." (Sir 26:12) He renders Genesis 2–3 (Sir 25:24) as "From woman sin had its beginning, and because of her we all die."

As the repayment burden became unbearable, the son and successor of Antiochus III, Seleucus IV Philopator ("Seleucus who loves his father") sent his minister, Heliodorus, to Jerusalem. The mission, based partly on recent espionage, was to steal the Jewish temple treasury.[4] Heliodorus thought he recognized an opportunity: He returned from Jerusalem to Seleucus IV and murdered him, briefly becoming emperor.[5] In the resulting mayhem, Antiochus IV Epiphanes, younger brother of Seleucus IV, seized power.[6] Antiochus IV removed Heliodorus and eventually killed an infant heir of Seleucus IV. In this way he became undisputed emperor in 175 BCE. Tired of the prior generation's setbacks, Antiochus IV initiated an 11-year crusade to restore his empire's prestige.

This included an aggressive Hellenizing campaign against his recent acquisition, Palestine's Jews. The Seleucid Empire had always pursued an active cultural war on its territories: their courts, civil service elite, and military leadership were Greek, the cities and commercial centers were infused with Greek businessmen, and the empire actively recruited Greek immigrants to press Greek culture and ideas into its territories. But gradual, piecemeal assimilation of the Jews was now not sufficient for Antiochus IV. His empire was in crisis, Palestine was in the capital's back yard, and Judea was associated with[7] monotheism and an air of cultural superiority/exclusiveness, ritualized in circumcision—things which were strange and offensive to Greek sensibilities.

The office of high priest, the chief political officer and religious official of Judea, was auctioned off by Antiochus Epiphanes to the highest Hellenizing bidder, going first to Jason (175–172 BCE), then Menelaus (172–162 BCE). As their Hellenized names suggest, their tenures were meant to pursue active assimilation of

---

4. This venture may be commemorated in Daniel 11:20, and is certainly commemorated in 2 Maccabees 3:2–3 and 21–28.

5. The lineal heir to the empire was being held in Rome as hostage for the war-reparation payments.

6. "Epiphanes" translates "God manifest," though he is also sometimes called Seleucus Epimanes, "Seleucus the Mad."

7. E.g., Elliott, *A Home for the Homeless*, 82.

Jews into Greek ways. Jason introduced and enforced many Greek customs, epitomized by his construction of a Greek gymnasium in Jerusalem. This new focal point of culture found resonance throughout the region when Jason physically reconstructed Jerusalem as a Greek-Aristotelian *polis*, establishing in stone and mortar the requirements of Aristotle's household codes. In fact, Jerusalem ceased to be Jerusalem; it was renamed *Antiochia* after the king. This was a deliberate renunciation by Jason of the political laws promulgated just a few years earlier by Antiochus III, who allowed Judea's polity to conform to the Torah rather than Aristotle.

Jason sent Menelaus to the emperor in 172 as a courier with tribute money. (Had he not read what happened when Heliodorus was sent as a financial emissary?) The gesture may have been calculated as a way to show loyalty to Hellenization, since Menelaus led a faction of hyper-Hellenizers called the *Tobiads*. If so, Jason made a miscalculation. The *Tobiads* had been looking for a way to displace Jason and, so they perceived, his lingering loyalty to the religion of the Jews.

In his errand to the emperor, Menelaus saw his opportunity to offer a bribe larger than Jason's. Thus he became the Jews' new high priest and chief political officer. As protection for Menelaus's return to Antiochia/Jerusalem, Antiochus sent an officer and troops to collect the bribe and assure an orderly transition of power. The payoff was financed in part by Menelaus's first official act as high priest: seizure and removal of the Temple's sacred vessels. His second act was to arrange the murder of the pre-Jason high priest Onias III, who had publicly exposed Menelaus's plundering of the Temple.

Menelaus continued to expropriate the Temple's remaining wealth. When a violent protest emerged, he persuaded Emperor Antiochus that his Jewish critics were actually motivated by a treasonous desire to return to the Ptolemaic Empire. Eventually the critics succeeded in proving their accusations against Menelaus. He responded by executing them.

Menelaus ruled for one turbulent decade, which included an attempt by Jason to return as high priest. That attempt resulted in a military campaign against Antiochia/Jerusalem by Emperor Antiochus, complete with a massacre of the city's people, destruction of the city walls, and seizure of the remaining Temple treasures. Menelaus and Antiochus then moved to fully Hellenize the last outpost of resistance, the worship practices of the Jews. Circumcision, possession of the sacred writings, and Temple festivals were all banned; worship of the Greek pantheon was made mandatory. In 167 BCE, the Temple was consecrated anew to the worship of Zeus. Just in case someone had missed their point, a new priesthood of Greeks was dispatched to Antiochia, and commenced sacrificing pigs on the Temple altar.

The Jewish Resistance

This series of events precipitated a sustained resistance movement that we now think of as the Maccabean War. A group calling itself the *Hasidim* ("the pious" or "the covenant faithful") became a seedbed of the resistance. The movement grew into a violent guerrilla conflict to expel the Greeks and their influence, centered around the Jewish priest Mattathias and his sons Judas, Simon, and Jonathan. When Mattathias was killed, Judas "the hammer" (*Judas Maccabeus*) assumed leadership.

By 164 BCE, Judas had reconquered the Temple and reconsecrated it. The resistance and rededication has ever since been celebrated in the annual feast of Hanukkah. (Jesus and his disciples of course observed Hanukkah, recorded in John 10.) Judas Maccabeus razed Antiochia and replaced it with a Jewish palace. His brother Jonathan served as the diplomatic arm of the insurrection, eventually sealing an alliance with Rome. In response, the Seleucids retreated to their capital at Syrian Antioch. For the time being, Rome had other distractions, and by 141 BCE, the rebels were left in charge of Judea.

Perhaps you were hoping that this would be a *Return of the Jedi* moment. Yet you sense down deep that the narrative arc is more like *Game of Thrones*. Unfortunately, there is not a happy ending. The descendants of Mattathias formed a dynastic monarchy, the Hasmonean Dynasty, which survived for just under eighty years—the first free Jewish rule in centuries, and the last free Jewish rule for millennia. Simon was given perpetual high priestly status, though he was not of the Zadok priesthood the *Hasidim* had fought to restore. Simon set out to concentrate power and wealth around his own aristocratic clique in Jerusalem. The *Hasidim,* whose love of law and piety had inspired the uprising, were locked out of power. Estranged from the temple's aristocrats, they eventually became the local synagogue-based Pharisee movement. They vied for influence in a three-way struggle with the temple-oriented Hasmonean aristocracy and the substantial population of Hellenized Jews.

The Hasmoneans and their high priests gradually descended into petty cruelty to maintain their status. For example, in 128 BCE, John Hycanus leveled the Samaritans' sanctuary on Mount Gerizim. Several decades later, Alexander Jannaeus (note his Hellenized name) perceived a challenge to his qualifications to be priest, and massacred 6,000 at the Feast of Tabernacles. He eventually crucified 800 Pharisees in a single year, in each case butchering their family before their eyes as they hung on a cross. (It was not only the Romans who used public crucifixions to terrorize opponents.) The Pharisees responded predictably by inciting hatred of this priesthood. When the Jewish Queen (141–67) Salome Alexandra (there's that name again!) rebalanced power toward the Pharisee party, they indulged in a violent retaliation.[8]

Though the origins of the New Testament-era Sadducee movement are obscure—we do not have any written records of their history or opinions, and know of them only from descriptions by their opponents—the Sadducee connections to aristocrats, temple life, and cultural accommodation suggest they are related to the Hasmonean aristocracy. Thus the New Testament's daily social landscape—Pharisees guarding observance of the law, Sadducees preserving their aristocratic influence, Essenes withdrawing from the Sadducees' abuse of the temple, and Zealots advocating

8. Did I mention that Salome's second husband had been Alexander Jannaeus, who so effectively *persecuted* Pharisees?!

a new Maccabean revolution—this entire social landscape was an echo of the events of the Hasmonean period, a daily reminder of the Jews' experience with Hellenization. This is further evidence that knowledge of Hellenistic ideas would have been a common, everyday experience in first-century Galilee and Judea.

Let us review. Alexander, the personal student of Aristotle, conquered his world as a missionary for Greek culture and philosophy. His successors went to great lengths to assure that Greek culture would dominate, particularly in the case of Palestine. By the first century CE, Jews like Peter lived with constant reminders of these attempts to Hellenize their culture—from speech and dress to their schooling in Jewish writings, from social structure and Samaritan encounters to annual religious festivals and debates about circumcision. Thus we have a great deal of indirect evidence that people like Peter would have been conversant in the contours of Greek civilization and philosophy. We will soon review the *direct* evidence that this familiarity would have included knowledge of Aristotle's household codes. But first we should briefly recount Rome's role in Hellenizing Palestine.

Rome arrives

As the Hasmoneans were busy suppressing their own countrymen and building a mini-empire for themselves, Rome was gradually expanding its empire eastward. For yet another time, Palestine sat awkwardly in an empire's crosshairs. Egypt and Syria were twin commercial, intellectual, and strategic prizes, and under the Roman military commander Pompey (106–48 BCE) Rome had a strategy: march through Asia Minor, capture the Seleucid capital at Syrian Antioch, march through Palestine, and capture Alexandria.

Pompey took Antioch in 64 BCE. Turning south, he freed the ten-city Greek federation just northeast of Galilee's border, the Decapolis, from the oppressive Hasmonean rule. He promised the Decapolis would never again have to submit to Jewish leadership. By 63 BCE, Pompey was in Jericho, on the doorstep of a Jewish civil war in Jerusalem between rivals for the crown. Unable to secure a firm commitment to a treaty, in a single day Pompey besieged Jerusalem, broke its defenses, killed the temple priests where they stood, and marched his Gentile boots into the Holy of Holies. Twelve thousand Jerusalem Jews lay dead.

As one might expect, Pompey chose a compliant high priest, killed the opposition's leadership, established confiscatory taxes, and left behind two Roman legions to keep the peace. He forced Palestine's Jews into ghettoes—Galilee, Jerusalem, and Jericho—giving the entire seacoast to Greek, Roman, and other foreign settlers who commenced the worship of a variety of pagan gods.

This Palestinian "peace treaty" was relaxed somewhat when the outnumbered forces of Julius Caesar defeated Pompey's army at Pharsalus in 48 BCE. For governor of Judea, Rome chose Antipater I, a prosperous, compliant Idumean from the wilderness south of Judea. He was conveniently non-Hasmonean; his parents were an Arab and an Idumean who had been forcibly converted to Judaism by Sadducees. Assassinated by a rival in 43 BCE, he was eventually replaced by his son, Herod the Great. Herod had grown up in Rome, received a complete Roman education, and become friends with Caesar's children. He successfully recaptured Jerusalem for Rome after the Persian invasion of 40 BCE, earning the title the Roman Senate had conferred: The King of the Jews.

One can appreciate his paranoia, this friend and toady of the distant Romans who was considered an alien interloper by the local aristocracy. His forty-year rule is littered with projects driven by this awkward situation. He constructed a fabulous new port city named for Caesar (Caesarea Maritima) on his Mediterranean coast, which had lacked a natural port. He saturated the new city with Greek-Roman cultural references—a theater, a hippodrome, an amphitheater, a dominating port-side temple dedicated to the worship of Caesar Augustus. Caesarea Maritima rivaled the best ports on the Mediterranean, and became the place from which Roman governors like Pontius Pilate would rule, climbing the road to Jerusalem only when necessary.

Herod also constructed a necklace of palaces and forts throughout his territory, strategically placed for maximal military use and, in the worst case, escape value. Herod arranged no less than 45 political assassinations of Hasmonean potential rivals, and killed two of his own sons for good measure. (In this he chose unwisely. It was a third son who was convicted two years later of trying to poison him.) In Jerusalem, Herod built a racetrack and Greek-Roman theaters laced with pagan cult practices (all alien to Jewish sensitivities), and of course upgraded his palaces. And (one blushes at his cynicism) Herod initiated—perhaps to shore up support among the traditionalists, perhaps merely to impress visitors—an extravagant, 83-year reconstruction of the Jerusalem temple.

Herod's reign briefly overlapped Jesus' lifetime. Upon Herod's death, his kingdom was split among three descendants, all of whom had been educated in Rome.

1. *Archelaus's* decade-long rule of Judea/Samaria/Idumea in the south was so harsh that the rebellions had to be suppressed by three Roman legions from Syria, who crucified 2,000 rebels. Augustus had had enough. He banished Archelaus to Gaul at the other end of the empire. For all but three of the next sixty years Judea/Samaria/Idumea came under direct Roman control through a succession of eleven appointed prefects and procurators. These included Pontius Pilate, 26–36 CE.

2. In the meantime, outside of Judea/Samaria/Idumea, *Herod Antipas* ruled Galilee in the north for forty years, constructing two Hellenistic capital cities (Sepphoris near Nazareth, and Tiberius, named for the emperor [14–37 CE], on the Sea of Galilee). Jesus and his father, as *tekton* craftsmen/contractors, may have worked on the construction of Sepphoris. As a slightly-older man, on trial for his life, Jesus majestically stares down Herod Antipas, refusing to even acknowledge this murderer of his cousin John.

3. *Philip* ruled the Hellenized, pacified, northeast corner of Herod the Great's lands, across the Jordan River from Galilee. There he constructed a new capital city on the Jordan,

naming it to simultaneously honor Caesar Augustus and himself: Caesarea Philippi.

Rome repurposes Aristotle's household code

The cozy relationship between the rulers of Palestine and the Emperors Augustus and Tiberius is important for our project, because with these emperors came a renewed emphasis on the historic household codes.

We know Aristotle's codes were a significant part of the prior three centuries' Hellenization of the world's cultures, because we find references to them (and to edited, adjusted versions) throughout the territories of the Hellenistic period. Unfortunately, our access to these post-Aristotle codes is very imperfect;[9] the next overview of post-Aristotle political theory comes during the reign of Augustus, at his initiative, from the pen of Arius Didymus.

Though he lived to see all of the conquests by his student Alexander, Aristotle never changed his views about the proper political ordering of society. His was a world of the *polis,* which was naturally limited in size, small enough to allow all of the *oikos* patriarchs to democratically govern in a single meeting place. This did not seem to allow for empire-building.

This concerned Augustus. It is a testament to the continuing influence of Aristotle's codes that Augustus felt obliged to construct some credible Hellenistic philosophical cover for his new empire. His friend and court philosopher, Arius Didymus, composed a retelling of Aristotle's household codes that would create a basis for political empire. Didymus does this in his *Epitome of Peripatetic Ethics and Politics* by reframing the relationship between household and *polis.* It all happens in two brief back-to-back analyses—a total of roughly two pages of text. In the opinion of many, these two short tracts are not mutually consistent.

---

9. "Our sources for Aristotelian political theory in the period after Alexander are extremely limited." (Nagel, "Aristotle and Arius Didymus on Household and *POLIS*," 198)

Aristotle rationalized his structures of *polis* and *oikos* as necessary pairings of complementary parts—city/estates, male/female, master/slave. Didymus deletes this rationale in his first discussion of households. In fact, in this first of his two household-definitions he side-steps the topic of slavery altogether. This allows him, like his great Jewish contemporary Philo, to picture the *polis* not as a *democratic counterbalance* to the non-democratic *oikos,* but instead as a natural *extension* of the non-democratic *oikos,* an extension without a natural geographic limit. For Didymus, the *polis* is just a grown-up *oikos.* These metaphoric households are free to go on getting bigger and bigger at various levels of the social hierarchy. This makes an empire into simply a very mature *oikos.* For Aristotle, this unthinkable logic would have made all citizens slaves of the state—which is not far from the Empire's intent.

Didymus's logic also allows the Emperor to be depicted as a super-*paterfamilias,* the patriarch of patriarchs, the father of his people. In 12 BCE, Augustus was proclaimed *Pontifex Maximus*—high priest—associating his gods with the state and, in effect, declaring him the divinely-sanctioned *paterfamilias* to the empire. This *paterfamilias* status was officially acknowledged in 2 BCE when he was designated *Pater patriae,* "super-paterfamilias," a designation he especially cherished and used in his consolidation of power.[10] From then on, opposition to the imperial version of the traditional household codes was, in effect, opposition to Caesar's right to rule.

Didymus's subtle shift of rationale not only allows the existence of empires; it allows tyranny within them. For Aristotle, there was a consensual relationship among equals in the *polis,* complemented by the *oikos's* monarchic relationship between fathers and children/slaves and aristocratic relationship between husbands and wives. With Didymus, monarchy can now serve as a model for the structure of the whole empire, since the emperor is now the great father of his people.

In his second definition of *oikos,* Didymus repeats, in very succinct form, Aristotle's household code *oikos* structure and

---

10. Elliott, *A Home for the Homeless,* 221.

hierarchy. This includes the natural rule of others by the husband, justified by his superior powers of deliberation. As in Aristotle, those powers are inferior in wives and absent in slaves. Like Aristotle, Arius gives no rationale for the natural status of slaves by convention. There is no discussion of the place of this household in a *polis*. There is no discussion of Aristotle's most basic claim, that participation in the *polis* by the *oikos* is an essential element of virtue and living the good life. Didymus's household could, conveniently enough, exist in any sort of state, including an empire.

Thus, though Didymus's household code makes some adjustments to Aristotle in order to license empire-building, his rationale, structure, and behavioral expectations for the household are essentially the same as Aristotle's. As in Aristotle, there is no reference to love (though there is a suggestion that households might form for reasons of companionship as well as commercial activity).

We have several reasons to think this work by Didymus was widely influential. It emerges as a formal treatise in an era in which philosophy was generally considered an acceptable pastime but did not produce much formal work; even Cicero did not produce a treatise by Greek standards. Didymus's adjustments to Aristotle are echoed in the work of the Jewish scholar Philo (25 BCE–50 CE, whereas Didymus died 10 BCE),[11] which may suggest that Didymus's work was quickly and successfully disseminated. And Didymus's work has survived, whereas other serious works of philosophy in Latin written by less influential authors are now lost, aside from their titles and authors' names. (From these lists we do know that Stoicism was not yet dominant, and Aristotelian thought was experiencing a revival.)

Especially relevant to our consideration of 1 Peter, which is addressed to territories in Asia Minor, is a cultural movement anticipated by Didymus's work: the emergence of the so-called Second Sophistic (roughly 60s–230 CE). This was a revival of interest in the classical Greek texts and traditions, reflected in the work of scholars like Lucian and Philostratus, the *Orations* of Dio Chrysostom and the letters of Pliny the Younger (both writing in Asia

11. For example, ibid., 173.

Minor's Bithynia early in the second century CE), the writings of Jewish scholars like Philo of Alexandria and Flavius Josephus.[12] These texts indicate that Aristotelian *oikos* language was fundamental to the vocabulary of economic and political discourse throughout the empire in this era, and that *oikos* was being used as an archetype for the full political order.[13] This implies Didymus's work, and its household-code framework, would have been common knowledge in the regions to which 1 Peter was addressed.[14]

It is worth noting that Didymus's literary *style* as well as his content may also serve as part of the cultural framework for the New Testament household codes:

> [Theses] proposed by Arius on household management and politics are compressed and complex, and their arrangement often involves a considerable degree of subtlety. Information is presented incrementally, with a minimum of argument. Sometimes what looks like a forthright statement of doctrine is subsequently modified—or virtually negated—by what follows.[15]

It would not be surprising to find a faithful reading of the New Testament codes might involve some reading between the lines.

Augustus's emphasis on household codes included several law initiatives. This gives us another indication of how deeply

12. For example, Bingham and Jefford, *Intertextuality in the Second Century*, 1–2.

13. Elliott, *A Home for the Homeless*, 179. The Aristotelian vision of *omonoia* among households was even actively promoted in Asia Minor, both in writing and through coins, as a pursuit of natural harmony and equilibrium that should rival the empire's *pax Romana* ideology. (Brent, "Ignatius of Antioch in Second Century Asia Minor," 70–71) Clement (Bishop of Rome, 88–99 CE) already testifies to the widespread influence of these Second Sophistic influences. (Ibid., 83–86) Scholars also find that the Second Sophistic movement—specifically its invocation of *oikos-polis* economic arrangements as truly natural and harmonious—significantly influenced the development of early Christian theology. See, e.g., Bingham and Jefford, *Intertextuality in the Second Century*.

14. Elliott, *A Home for the Homeless*, 180.

15. Nagle, "Aristotle and Arius Didymus on Household and *POLIS*," 200.

household codes were embedded in the general culture. While the *paterfamilias* was still responsible for the life and reputation of the household, his local life-and-death authority over the extended household became limited by law, and he was encouraged to make major decisions collaboratively with his peers and wife. At the same time, harsh adultery laws, precipitated by Augustus's concern that the Empire was declining into self-indulgence and debauchery, allowed the *paterfamilias* to kill adulterous daughters and their partners and, in some cases, adulterous wives.

Augustus, apparently reacting to liberating influences (especially concerning the roles of women) and a falling birth rate (which he attributed to moral degeneracy and personal selfishness) promulgated the *lex Julia de Maritandis Ordinibus* (18 BCE) and *lex Julia de Adulteriis Coercendis* (around 17 BCE). Augustus sought to corral marriage within social class constraints (with the effect of encouraging concubinage), penalize the inheritance rights of the unmarried, and require remarriage of widows and the divorced. He encouraged public dress codes for women, and directed charges of adultery (which are only brought against women) toward public legal proceedings rather than *paterfamilias* tribunals. Adultery brought the penalty of banishment to islands, though a father might kill guilty daughters and their partners, could kill his own adulterous partner in some cases, and was required to divorce an adulterous wife.

This apparently promoted four ends: Increasing the power of the empire relative to the independent *paterfamilias*, encouraging Augustus's vision of morality, reducing the number of honor killings among *patres familias*, and providing a convenient charge—adultery—that might be used to demote powerful women. Augustus did exactly this against his only child in 2 BCE and, later, against her oldest daughter. A revolt against these laws' effects on inheritance led to several adjustments in the *lex Papia Poppaea* (9 CE), and the laws were later adjusted further in practice, all leading to a gradual expansion of magistrates' prerogatives over those of the traditional *paterfamilias*. The magnitude and timing of the practical effects of these changes in various parts of the empire is a matter of debate, but at the least they demonstrate that Aristotelian categories of household and *paterfamilias* were common, everyday notions in the first-century empire.

To summarize, we know that in the New Testament era, Palestine was governed by leaders eager to please Rome. We have seen that, from several angles, engaging the household codes was a part of pleasing Rome, and formed part of the everyday cultural fabric. In fact, we know from a variety of sources that the household codes were such a significant element of loyalty to the empire that religious movements felt obliged to take public positions concerning them.

Direct evidence: No one writes about things of which they are unaware

In addition to this indirect evidence that people like Peter would be familiar with the contours of Greek thought, what direct evidence can be cited that Jesus' disciples were indeed familiar with the household codes?

The best evidence must surely be the existence of household codes in the documents that Jesus' followers penned. Why else would the New Testament contain this peculiar form of ethical instruction—pairings of husband/wife, parent/child, and master/slave—unless it was a widely-known formula? And where else would this formula come from, if not the Aristotelian tradition?[16]

We have several overt references to Hellenism's household codes in the New Testament canon—in Ephesians, Colossians, 1 Peter, and perhaps also 1 Timothy and Titus.[17] They all seem to address the classic Aristotelian ideas rather than any of Arius's revisions. Surely their existence argues the codes were familiar to

---

16. In his extensive review of the potential influences on the New Testament household codes, Balch (*Let Wives be Submissive,* 49) finds that Aristotle's is the most important parallel.

17. Eph 5:21—6:9; Col 3:18—4:1; 1 Pet 2:13—3:7; 1 Tim 2:1–2, 8–15, 3:1–5, 8–13, 6:1–2; Titus 2:1–10.

the recipients of the letters, and thus would be familiar to a leader like Peter.

One might argue the New Testament documents in which we find household codes were primarily addressed to Greek-speaking Gentiles. If that is so (and this is not a given), perhaps the codes were known to Gentiles, but not to Palestinian Jews like Peter?

I believe we have evidence within the New Testament canon, in Matthew's gospel, that Jews in particular were conversant with the Aristotelian household codes. It is generally agreed Matthew's primary audience was Jewish readers. Matthew makes constant reference to the Hebrew Scriptures, and portrays Jesus as reliving—righteously—the history of the Jews, and thus satisfying the standards of the covenants on behalf of God's errant people. The book opens with an extended Jewish genealogy. Then there is a captivity in Egypt, then wandering in the wilderness for forty time periods, then the giving of law on a mountaintop. Jesus is portrayed as the promised new Moses, and also the promised new David of the new covenant. In fact the gospel is, like the Torah, organized into five sections. Each ends with a compendium of Jesus' teachings, followed by the formula "When Jesus had completed saying these things . . . "

The book opens with the questions that had troubled Jews in Palestine for generations: Who is the true king? When will God deliver on the promise to return to the Temple, fill it with glory, and live with his people? What will that reign be like? The questions are raised in classically Jewish fashion—through narrative storytelling.

The book's fourth section—Matthew 19–25—directly addresses the nature of the new David's kingdom. Matthew opens this section on the messianic kingdom with a household code. It is a code that subverts the classic Aristotelian code, and once again it is presented through the medium of storytelling. The author takes the prevailing secular household code to be the epitome of Caesar's kingdom and the kingdom of his local puppets, and portrays the nature of Jesus' kingdom by contrast, offering an upended household code. (Mark 10, the gospel generally believed to represent Peter's witness, also records this.)

First the husband-wife relationship is addressed. Jesus walks to Judea, where he is met by Pharisees. They test him with a question about divorce—a question that appears to be deliberately ambiguous: "Is it lawful for a man to divorce his wife for any cause?" This might mean "is divorce *ever* permissible?" Or it could mean "may a man leave his wife for any reason at all that he finds personally compelling?" Or it might mean "Tell us which of the many rationales for divorce in Hellenized culture are consistent with our interpretation of Torah." Or it may mean "Doesn't Torah present marriage as essentially a property issue—maintaining clear lines of inheritance and clear title to the woman's right to payment if divorced? It can't be an issue of personal devotion, right? Moses gave the law against adultery, but he also had several wives." Or it could suggest "Hellenizers (referencing Demosthenes) seem to think there are different sorts of women—some you marry for reasons of property, some you have intimacy with for reasons of enjoyment, some you discuss ideas with at the gymnasium.[18] Isn't that about right? And if your property-relationship woman fails you in property issues, isn't it OK to walk away from that contract?"

Jesus answers that Torah *opens* with teaching that provides the context for the rest of Torah's law: From the beginning there is just one kind of woman, not three, and when you marry a woman the marriage is about becoming more than a joint commercial venture. In fact, the intent is to become a single, integrated entity, in which the distance enshrined in Aristotle's code between husband and wife becomes unthinkable.

The Pharisees seem to have anticipated this answer, and have a ready comeback: "Then why does Torah treat divorce like a property issue? Just give a receipt so the divorce is publicly observed, and you've clarified the germane inheritance and ownership issues." Jesus insists this provision was a matter of accommodation.

---

18. Not that these were hermetically-sealed independent groups. In classical Greece, women of respectable reputation were excluded from the "symposia" dinner parties that were the focus of propertied (male) citizens' social life.

Personal relationship is primary, not property relationship. Divorce comes under the rubric of adultery law, not property law.

Next, in Matthew's account, comes the issue of parents and children. When people bring their children to Jesus to be prayed over, the disciples speak sternly to them. They shoo the children away. You can imagine them fuming: "Jesus is a very important man. Why he's more important than any *paterfamilias*, and (so says Aristotle) important men do not waste their time on little children. Important men like us are harsh with children, to prepare them for leadership." Jesus again subverts the culture's default economics text, saying pointedly that even the *little* children should be brought: It is *to such as these* that the kingdom *belongs*. This is clearly a striking departure from the kingdom of Aristotle and Caesar.

So we've had a story about husbands and wives, and a story about parents and children. Now you are expecting a story about masters and slaves, right? And what is the next story?

Jesus is approached by a *paterfamilias,* someone who had inherited at an early age and was now deeply conflicted about his vocation. He comes asking what good deed he must do to have eternal life. We are told in the parallel account (Mark 10) that he ran up to Jesus and knelt down with his question—striking humility and intensity of purpose for a *paterfamilias*. We are also told Jesus felt a deep affection for this man; perhaps we can hear Jesus responding with a gentle twinkle in the eye. He says: "Well, you must know the commandments," and then recites the six commandments.

Six, not ten? He leaves out the commandments concerning honoring God and coveting. You can sense Jesus hoping that this promising lad will have an *a-ha* moment. He comes so close: "I have kept all these; what do I still lack?" Then Jesus points out the obvious. The *paterfamilias* must face his struggles with avarice and true piety. The young man "went away grieving, for he had many possessions." The word used for *grieving* is a strong word, once again displaying behavior one would not expect in public of a *paterfamilias* unless the trauma is very deep. One can picture the heartbreak as the *paterfamilias* gets up from his knees, awkwardly hesitates, glances down, and slowly walks away.

This is a story about a master and a slave. This young *paterfamilias,* in the eyes of Caesar's kingdom a master, is in Jesus' eyes a slave. He is possessed by his possessions. Jesus' household code has completely inverted Aristotle's.

On two occasions the disciples express incredulity at Jesus' teachings, and both of these take place in this short chapter. The apostles are dumbfounded that Jesus is inverting Aristotle's code concerning marriage, then dumbfounded that he does the same thing concerning wealth and possessions. The appearance of a household code in this gospel indicates Aristotle's codes were well known in Jewish circles; the disciples' reaction to Jesus' teaching suggests household-code logic had become deeply ingrained.

In both Matthew and Mark this household code is followed by an epilogue. James and John, who along with Peter form Jesus' innermost circle, approach Jesus privately (apparently egged on by their mother) with a request: when you finally come into your kingdom, when you become the super-*paterfamilias,* please promise that these two sons will be your second-in-command, your under-*paterfamilias.* (Among other things, this was a tremendous slap in the face to Peter, who had clearly been functioning as lead disciple.) When the other ten hear about this, they are indignant. Jesus' comments are remarkable:

> You know that the rulers of the Gentiles lord it over them, and their great ones are tyrants over them. [26]It will not be so among you; but whoever wishes to be great among you must be your servant (*diakonos*), [27]and whoever wishes to be first among you must be your slave (*doulos*); [28]just as the Son of Man came not to be served but to serve, and to give his life a ransom for many. (Matthew 10, NRSV)

Once again, Jesus inverts the *oikos* structure. He will be servant of servants, not *paterfamilias* of *patres familias.*

Peter the Wise

I'd like to consider one last objection to the notion that Peter could have penned a treatise on the Aristotelian household codes. Doesn't the New Testament tell us that prosecutors at Peter's first trial noted that he and John were courageous but "unschooled, ordinary men?" (Acts 4:13)

Let us lay aside the fact that correspondence in this era was often written by a lead author working with a drafting team or professional scribe. Even the learned Paul acknowledges such co-authorship, and in Peter's case this might allow a more refined use of Greek language and ideas than Peter might muster in isolation. Let us also lay aside the suggestion, common among New Testament scholars, that 1 Peter was written after Peter's death by a circle of his companions, applying Peter's witness to situations Peter did not personally encounter. So consider the strongest version of this objection concerning Peter's "unschooled, ordinary" background: assume Peter wrote 1 Peter and worked entirely alone. Several considerations are important:

1. The comments about Peter's educational background in Acts 4:13 come after Peter's self-defense at a capital trial. Hellenistic culture had, for half a millennium, been obsessed with the mastery of refined rhetoric initiated by the Sophists, particularly in life-and-death legal proceedings. This theme was receiving fresh attention around the time of Peter's trial, in the era of the so-called "Second Sophistic."

   Now contrast Peter's defense (Acts 4) with the elegant rhetorical defense (Acts 24) offered by the Apostle Paul, well-trained in Hellenistic culture, philosophy, and rhetoric:

   > Peter: "Well, since I have been arrested for helping some-one who was sick, which is a *requirement* of your law, let me proclaim to all of the people *you* claim to rule that this kindness was done by the name of Jesus, whom you killed after a show trial just like this one." (That's my personal translation, but I think it's a nice one.)

Paul: "I cheerfully make my defense, knowing that for many years you have been a judge over this nation . . . " This introduction is followed by a careful catalogue of the things Paul did and did not do, emphasizing points of agreement with his accusers wherever possible; he also gently points out his accusers have not shown up for the trial. In his second hearing he goes on to discuss the legal principles of justice and self-control at stake in his trial.

You can see Peter is breaking the rules of polite company. The New American Standard Bible's characteristically literal translation of the prosecutors' reaction, to which I've added some parenthetical translation suggestions, serves us well here:

"As they (the prosecutors) observed the confidence of the apostles, and understood (the tense suggests they knew this before the trial) that (in contrast to Peter's level of confidence) they were uneducated and untrained (in the rhetorical arts of capital self-defense), they were amazed (at how well Peter was defending himself), and began to recognize them as having been with Jesus (because Jesus was also brilliant, and because Jesus offered a similar "unpolished," non-Hellenistic defense at his own trial).[19]

The point of this Acts 4 passage is Peter's *natural intelligence*, not his lack of higher education. With one unrehearsed sentence Peter had stumped a room full of well-prepared, Hellenized legal scholars. You can now begin to hear the gears spinning in the prosecutors' brains: *Oh no! We've seen this movie before! We reacted to Jesus' similar defense in a similar situation by ramming through a false conviction. That turned out horribly! What are we going to do with these fellows!?"* As the text reports, the prosecutors were speechless. They finally dismissed the defendants from the room, to develop Plan B.

19. Note the similar reaction, by some of the same people, when Jesus presented rhetoric at the Temple late in his ministry during the Feast of Booths, recorded in John 7:15 (NRSV): "The Jews were astonished at it, saying, 'How does this man have such learning, when he has never been taught?'"

Peter certainly displays a familiarity with the Scriptures similar to Jesus', and so it is reasonable to think Peter had received a similar formal education in reading Hebrew. The comment that both men were "unschooled" likely represents a lack of formal education on the Greek model, which was standardized and well established throughout the Empire. That curriculum consisted of about seven years of elementary school (reading, writing, music, athletics), then tutoring in poetry and grammar, capped off (for some) by an advanced formal education in rhetoric and philosophy.

2. Peter and several of the other disciples came from families in the fishing profession. Post-enlightenment observers may hear this and think, "ah yes, those simple-minded indigent fishermen." That is not an accurate portrayal. In the first century, about half of the Empire's population lived at or below subsistence, usually by scrounging for day-to-day laboring work, sometimes gathering in a town center each day and hoping to be chosen from the lineup for manual labor. They were peasants with small and unproductive plots of land, unattached widows, orphans, the disabled, prisoners, small-time merchants or traders or tavern owners, under-provisioned serfs, or people who were for other reasons blocked from the means to make their own way in the world. We know from archaeological evidence that they were chronically malnourished and had very little in the way of a safety net.

The well-off—imperial elites, senatorial families, provincial officials, some retired military officers, estate owners, a few merchants, and some particularly fortunate freed persons—made up only 3 to 4 percent of the population. That leaves about 40 percent of the population as non-elite and regularly employed, with some prospect of saving or investing—some merchants and traders, some artisans, some veterans, some farmers and wage-earners. Thus home ownership and participation in a profession like fishing—which required skill, knowledge, and an outlay of scarce capital—probably put a family in roughly the top third of the income distribution.[20] This probably explains why the families of the disciples were financially able to release their sons from productive labor for three years while they studied with Jesus.

3. I will grant you in the gospels the disciples' mental acuity does not always inspire confidence.[21] The disciples often seem to miss the point of Jesus' teaching, and they are sometimes too ashamed of their immature actions to even speak of them to Jesus. They are petrified by a windstorm on an inland lake, even though many of them come from families that ply the lake for a living. Jesus' patience sometimes seems to boil off, and we are left with an exasperated savior.[22] On the other hand, we also sometimes see Peter saving the day with an insight the others have missed.

    These phenomena may have to do with the age profile of the disciples.[23] It is likely that many of Jesus' inner-circle of long-term disciples were, like the followers of most rabbis, chosen from young men in their early teens, as they completed their synagogue education. Jesus' call to "follow me" was a phrase generally used by rabbis offering potential students a long-term discipleship. At early-teen ages parents may be willing to let a son leave the family enterprise to receive an education, and the young men have the liberty to go because they do not yet have responsibility for feeding their own children. In the gospels, Jesus is generally called by titles (master, Rabbi) that indicate he has accepted the disciples as his students, and he generally calls them by titles consistent with their standing as his students (learners, lads). The school seems to have settled in particular places at some times (John 6:59, Matthew 5–7), and at other times seems to be an itinerant clinical experience. Most of the life of this community of

20. These reconstructions are drawn from Longenecker, *Remember the Poor*.

21. For examples, see Mark 9:5–6, Matthew 16:22–24, John 13:8–10, Acts 10:14 and 12:9.

22. For example, Mark 9:14–19, Matthew 16:5–12.

23. See, e.g., Cary and Cary, "How Old were Christ's Disciples?" for a long-lived analysis of the disciples' ages.

learners appears to take place in a small geographic territory within Galilee, with occasional short trips to Jerusalem or areas near Galilee.

Peter is the only disciple of whom we have a clear indication of marriage. It seems likely that the typical age at marriage for men was around 18, and that the typical man did indeed marry. Even an extended tutorial education (like the disciples' sojourn with Jesus) would usually be ending by around that same age.

So it seems likely the gospels record a ministry by Jesus to a fairly large group that, unique to his ministry at the time, included women in the itinerant school. Among the inner circle of twelve, echoing the number of Israel's tribes, it seems likely that many were teenagers, and that Jesus particularly relied upon a somewhat older disciple, Peter. Little wonder that the disciples sometimes seem immature and distractable in the gospels, yet are able to eventually lead a world-changing movement.

4

Peter's Dissident Correspondence

ARISTOTLE LIVED A VERY public life of great influence, and in its wake we have a substantial amount of information about his thought and personal history—even after losing a majority of his writings to the ravages of time. Things are different with the Christian apostles. Of the twelve whom Jesus specially commissioned to carry on his work, only three of them (at most) committed anything to writing. In the case of Peter, the universally-acknowledged leader of the group, we have at most about 2800 words in English translation from his own pen (fewer than one-third the words in the prior chapter of this book), plus some anecdotal narratives about Peter in a few of the other books of the Bible. If Aristotle's mind is difficult to enter because of the complexity of the witnesses, Peter's is difficult for just the opposite reason.

Who wrote 1 Peter?

Yes, this question sounds a lot like "Who's buried in Grant's tomb?" First Peter opens, like other New Testament and Roman first-century letters, with the name of the author—in this case, "Peter, an apostle of Jesus Christ." That would seem to settle the matter. And for centuries it did, though not as immediately as one might think. There was a long initial period of culturally-inclusive investigation and reflection on questions of authorship and content concerning the books that became the New Testament. That process lasted several centuries, and was conducted by people who were closer to ancient literature and its conventions than we are. It resulted in widespread acceptance of the letter as coming from Peter, Jesus' disciple.

Yet for the better part of the last two centuries the academic field of New Testament Studies has poured a great deal of energy into questions of authorship, underlying sources, and the function of books like 1 Peter in the life of their original community of faith. This academic work is by nature speculative, subject to swings of consensus and interpretation. To appreciate the current state of affairs, we must temporarily broaden our vision to include all of the New Testament books.

There is a scholarly consensus that some early letters attributed to Paul are genuinely the work of Paul. These include Romans, 1 and 2 Corinthians, Galatians, Philippians, Philemon, and probably 1 Thessalonians. The other New Testament letters signed by "Paul" are, to varying extents, often considered pseudepigraphical.

This does not necessarily signal the death of the letters' authority. Pseudepigraphy was not that uncommon in parts of the ancient world in some eras, and does not necessarily suggest an unseemly attempt to mislead.[1] "Authorship" and "authority" are related words; there seems to be evidence that, at least in some instances in the ancient world, a document drafted by faithful followers of a deceased teacher might have been received as bearing the teacher's authority, and thus *authored* by him or her, even though it was not *written* by him or her. The named author had been surrounded by a trusted circle, who now aimed to faithfully record their teacher's wisdom (much of which may have never been reduced to writing), or faithfully apply their teacher's known viewpoints to new situations that had emerged after the teacher's death. So pseudepigraphy does not imply inconsistency with the named author. In a manner of speaking, even those who are quite hesitant to allow this principle concerning the Pauline letters are simultaneously admitting it for the entire New Testament: Jesus

1. E.g., Fiorenza, *1 Peter,* 22.

did not write anything down, so far as we know, but the apostolic writing of his faithful followers has historically been received as bearing his authority, with Jesus as the received author. Thus Mark the evangelist, believed to be collaborating with Peter to write his gospel, begins his gospel not with "The Gospel of Mark," or even "The Gospel of Peter," but "The Gospel of Jesus."

The modern judgment that some books are pseudepigraphical is largely based on differences (in language, rhetorical style, and topics addressed) from letters known to be written by the named author, or (in cases where no known writing exists) based on an argument that some particular book could not have been written during the named author's lifetime. For example, some argue the earlier letters of Paul address specific situations in particular churches, whereas later pseudo-Pauline letters concern big-picture, enduring topics—topics that may have taken on added urgency after the deaths of the first generation of apostles. Some buttress this argument with the notion that the earlier letters seem to express urgency concerning the imminent return of Jesus, whereas the later books sometimes may argue against (some forms of) this same sense of urgency.

Out of such considerations, the New Testament's gospels, Pastoral Epistles, and General Epistles—that is, nearly everything but six or seven of Paul's letters—are often thought of as late first-century (or later) works, authored after the deaths of (at least most of) the apostles.

So who wrote 1 Peter? Historically the letter was considered to be penned by Peter while in Rome (5:13), likely in some leadership position there, very likely during the rule of Nero (54–68 CE), probably in the early 60s. The letter was widely received as authentic and authoritative; 1 Peter and 1 John were the only general epistles that were never contested in either the western or eastern territories of the church.[2]

Modern scholars have questioned this. They point out, as I am arguing in this book, that the author of the letter understood Hellenistic philosophy and had some substantial intellectual gifts. The

2. Witherington, *Invitation to the New Testament*, 307.

author's dexterity with Greek sources, the quality of the reasoning, and the quality of the written Greek suggest this. Many have argued this would have been beyond the ken of Peter from Galilee.

Others have suggested the "fiery ordeal" which Peter references, and the sufferings "throughout the world" (at 5:9), must correspond to an organized empire-wide persecution—something more widespread than Nero's tantrums. The first candidate for this might be the harassment of the church under Domitian. Peter is believed to have died in 64 CE during Nero's persecutions in Rome, but Domitian did not become emperor until 81 CE, and his harassments commenced around 93 CE. Others believe the argument of 1 Peter shows familiarity with and dependence upon the Pastoral Epistles and other works believed to have been written after Peter's death. Yet others find it odd that Peter of Galilee would quote the Septuagint rather than the Hebrew Scriptures, and would never reference personal details about his time with Jesus.

At this point a special note about the possibility of coauthorship is in order. We know the use of a scribal amanuensis for dictation, copy editing, and other collaborative writing services was widespread. Though Paul knew Greek well, the Pauline letters acknowledge a circle of colleagues—some as collaborators, some as scribes, some as delivery agents with the authority to expound and interpret the letters to the recipient churches. These include Silas (a nickname for Sylvanus), Mark, Phoebe, Timothy, Tertius, Barnabas, Priscilla, Tychicus, Luke, Aristarchus, Demas, and Aquila. Paul appears to have dictated much of his writing to scribes, and sometimes draws attention to the fact by writing the last lines in his own hand, mentioning this so the force of the gesture will not be lost as letters are recopied. In the case of Romans, the scribe Tertius is allowed to step out of character and jot a personal greeting, an act of humility on the part of the named author. The historian Josephus, who came from Jerusalem but wrote in Rome, used an amanuensis. Even the great Roman orator Cicero appears to have employed his amanuensis, Tiro, for dictation and copy editing.

So could Peter have written 1 Peter? The image of Peter working alone and in isolation raises more difficulties than if Peter were working with a team of colleagues. It seems very unlikely this first-among-apostles could not have arranged for coauthorship or scribal support from someone more fluent in Greek, if Peter was indeed not a native speaker. The book does comment, at 5:12, that (rendered literally) "*dia* Sylvanus to you . . . *dia* a few I have written." The NRSV renders this "Through Silvanus . . . I have written this short letter . . ." The ESV: "By Silvanus . . . I have written briefly to you . . ."

The preposition *dia* has, like many prepositions, a significant lexical range, as you can see by its use twice in this sentence to communicate what might be rather different things. Used with the genitive (as in both cases here) it can mean through/by the agency of, with/as a means of, or through/along (marking extension). Those skeptical of coauthorship take *dia Sylvanus* as an endorsement of Sylvanus's physical *delivery* of the book, not a reference to his assistance in composing it.[3] On the other hand, endorsement of the deliverer would certainly signal Peter's confidence in Sylvanus's reading of the letter and expounding/fielding of questions about it, and *dia could* signify Sylvanus has also been the copy editor or collaborator. Saying "I have written briefly through Sylvanus" seems an odd phrase to include if Sylvanus is merely the delivery boy; in that case a verb for "send," as in Acts 15:22–23 and two of Ignatius's letters from a few years later, would seem more likely. And why would the writer insert a comment merely to endorse a delivery boy? That would seem useful only if the recipients are skeptical, suspecting this delivery is a forgery and requiring some assurance from the author. But if this were in fact a forgery that is grasping for authenticity by including such a phrase, why would a skeptical recipient be persuaded? The endorsement of the carrier would also be a part of the forgery.

Also note Sylvanus's non-Hebrew name, the name of the Roman deity of fields and woods. He is a Roman citizen (according to Acts 16:37, which uses the shortened familiar form of his name, Silas). Silas is identified by Paul as his cowriter in 1 Thessalonians. Silas carried the instructions to the Gentiles in the church at Antioch after the great convocation in Jerusalem in 49 CE; identified

---

3. See, e.g., Richards, "Silvanus was not Peter's Secretary."

as a "leader among the brothers" and "a prophet" (Acts 15:22), his commission was not only to read the instructions but to say "much to encourage and strengthen the believers." (Acts 15:32) Silas and Mark (who is also named in 1 Peter as a colleague) were chosen by Paul and Barnabas as companions on missionary trips among the Gentiles. All of these select roles for Silas (and Mark) would be quite unexplainable if they lacked strong facility in the Greek language.

If the presence of an amanuensis makes it more credible that *Peter* may be the author of 1 Peter, there are additional reasons to lean in this direction. Though the author does not reference personal interactions with Jesus, he certainly reveals a deep familiarity with Jesus' words. First Peter's similarities to Paul's themes would be expected from personal contact (recorded in Acts, and likely repeated in Rome in the early 60s CE). The Pastoral Epistles could resemble 1 Peter because 1 Peter came first. In fact, 1 Peter's writing resonates not only with Paul and the Pastoral Epistles, but also with the Synoptic Gospels, Hebrews, and James—with virtually the entire New Testament witness. This is what one might expect when the leader of the disciples writes to the church at large. First Peter's rhetoric also resonates with the recorded words and thoughts of Peter in Acts. And 1 Peter was attested as Peter's own work by two nearly-contemporary sources (2 Peter and Clement).

Regarding the book's familiarity with Greek ideas and language, as I have argued in the last chapter, Peter and his companions likely had a substantial latent understanding of Greek philosophy and culture. The "fiery ordeal" and similar references throughout the book seem to reference the daily marginalization of and hostility toward Christians, not a widespread imperial persecution.[4] In fact, though there are some widespread harassments, true generalized imperial persecution probably does not emerge until around 251 CE under Decius, far too late to be referenced by this book.

---

4. The verbs at 2:12, 3:3, 3:16, and 4:14 suggest verbal abuse and social pressure, not physical mistreatment or legal action. (Elliott, *1 Peter*, 80) Fiorenza concludes (*1 Peter*, 28) that "virtually all recent interpreters agree that 1 Peter does not refer to an Empire-wide persecution of Christians but rather describes the situation of the recipients as harassment, social ostracism and slander of Christians on a local level."

Finally, the book begins with a sequential list of regions to which it will be delivered. They are ordered in a geographic circle, as if in the order to be visited by the letter carrier.[5] Pontus and Cappadocia were administratively joined by CE 63–64, then Cappadocia to Galatia by 72. Unless the author is referring to older, smaller nationalities within the administrative districts set by Rome, this would seem to place the date of composition in the early 60s, under Nero but probably before his persecutions.

To summarize, it is fair to say in the current culture of New Testament scholarship the authorship of this book is contested. No firm consensus exists. The authorship issue may not be crucial to the details of our study, but it will be helpful to work from some hypothesis about authorship, even as we may hold that hypothesis with a gentle grip. Adopting the convention that Peter is indeed the author will actually make it a bit more difficult for me to persuade you of my position, so that seems a polite thing to do. We could do worse than accept the advice of Benedict XVI on this matter:

> Peter the Apostle is speaking but the exegetes tell us: it is impossible for this Letter to have been written by Peter because the Greek is so good that it cannot be the Greek of a fisherman from the Sea of Galilee. And it is not only the language — the syntax is excellent — but also the thought which is already quite mature, there are actual formulas in which the faith and the reflection of the Church are summed up . . . Peter himself — that is, the Letter — gives us a clue, for at the end of the writing he says I write to you: "By Silvanus" . . . Then I think it is important that in the conclusion of the Letter Silvanus and Mark are mentioned, two people who were also friends of St Paul. So it is that through this conclusion the worlds of St Peter and St Paul converge: there is no

5. Since some of this itinerary parallels some of the groups present for Peter's Pentecost sermon in Acts 2, it has been suggested that these churches were initiated by pilgrims returning from those Pentecost events (e.g., Elliott, *1 Peter,* 64), that perhaps Peter and his wife, in their itinerant ministry mentioned elsewhere in the New Testament, made a follow-up visit to this region, and that Peter is now writing a follow-up letter.

exclusive Petrine theology as against a Pauline theology, but a theology of the Church ... [6]

Let us be content to refer to this book as Peter's own work. Regarding the believability of the other New Testament documents—such as the references to Peter's life in the gospels and Acts—this is not the place to rehearse an extended review of the last two centuries' debates about authorship and reliability. If time allowed, you would find me making the same sorts of affirmations about the rest of the New Testament's witness that I have made for 1 Peter. I will therefore refer to the New Testament documents as if they are reliable, and those who are not able to share this conviction will be able to sift my conclusions accordingly.

Peter: Fisherman, Disciple, Apostle

Peter's call and new name

The gospels tell us of Jesus' decision to call his first inner-circle students, including one *Simōn bar Yōna*, Simon son of Jonah, a fisherman working in *Bethsaida* ("house of fishing") on the Sea of Galilee. Jesus also calls the brothers James and John, Peter's business partners (according to Luke) who are still work associates of their father Zebedee (according to Matthew). Jesus nicknames James and John the "sons of thunder"; at one point they offer to call down brimstone on an inhospitable village. One wonders what the Monday morning staff meetings were like at their fishing enterprise.

Jesus' introduction to these fishermen comes through Simon's brother (and fourth business partner) Andrew, a follower of Jesus' cousin, John "the Baptizer." At about the same time, Jesus also seeks out and calls Philip, also of Bethsaida, who seeks out his close friend Nathaniel/Bartholomew from Cana—a ten-mile walk west of Bethsaida, quite near Nazareth.

In sum, the first six of the twelve apostles all grew up within a half-day's walk of the Hellenized regions just east of Galilee—the

---

6. Benedict XVI, "*Lectio Divnia* of the Holy Father Benedict," n.p.

Tetrarchy of Herod Philip II to the northeast, the Decapolis to the southeast. These disciples lived and worked on the routes by which Philip's territory traded with the Mediterranean and communicated with the Hellenized Galilean centers Sepphoris and Tiberius. It seems very likely these disciples' work would have sometimes been conducted in Greek,[7] the settled common language of business throughout the eastern Mediterranean region. Most of the action in the gospels appears to take place within just a few miles of these disciples' home towns, with forays eastward and westward into Hellenized, Greek-speaking territory (Tyre, Sidon, Caesarea Philippi, and elsewhere). In the Gospels the communication of Jesus and his disciples with these populations seems to have been effortless, conducted without translators.

It certainly appears Jesus and at least some of the disciples were literate in Hebrew, and thus almost certainly literate in the more commonly-used Aramaic. Men who could not read the Hebrew Torah were not allowed to teach in synagogues, as Jesus frequently does. We cannot know for sure if the disciples' Greek capacity would have been primarily spoken, or would have extended to literacy, but much scholarship argues that Galilee's bilingualism was so pervasive Jesus and people like him must have known Greek, and finds parallels between Jesus' style and thought processes and those of Hellenized culture.[8] And note Philip's Hellenized name—the name of Alexander the Great's father, and also of the contemporary political leader in the Hellenized Tetrarchy. Andrew, Peter's brother, also bears a Greek name, from *andreas,* meaning "manly." Philip and Andrew are portrayed in the Gospels as natural go-betweens for Greek-speakers (e.g., John 12). This certainly suggests Peter's brother and at least one other disciple had significant abilities in Greek.

In the gospel narratives, Peter's home seems to be near Capernaum, Jesus' adopted home town. Bethsaida and Capernaum lie

---

7. See, e.g., Freyne, *Galilee from Alexander the Great to Hadrian 323 BCE to 135 CE,* 139–41; Witherington, *Invitation to the New Testament,* 45.

8. For example, Dormeyer, *The New Testament Among the Writings of Antiquity,* 34, 57.

near the border between Herod's Galilee and Phillip's Gaulanitis. It has been suggested this choice of a home base was a strategic decision. Nazareth was roughly thirty miles westward in the hills, midway between the Sea of Galilee and the Mediterranean, just a walk from Herod's capital Sepphoris with no clear escape route. But from Capernaum one could slip across the border if Herod reprised the hostility he had shown to Jesus' cousin, John the Baptizer. From the beginning, Peter was the associate leader of a movement that involved giving up comforts and constantly looking over your shoulder at potential persecution.

Peter is the only apostle known to be married during the years with Jesus, and we are told he owned his own boat (from which Jesus sometimes preached). By contrast, James and John appear to be apprentices in the family fishing business. As I have suggested earlier, this places Peter in a relatively stable social position, as the archeological evidence from his hometown confirms.[9] He frequently displays leadership capacities, even if they are sometimes impulsive, not yet wizened by age and experience. He is always named in the "inner" inner circle of three apostles, and famously leads the entire movement in his recognition that Jesus was indeed the Messiah foretold.

At just that moment (related in Mark 8 and Matthew 16) Jesus coins a nickname pun: *Petros* in Greek, *Peter* in English. "You are *Petros* ("Rock"), and on this *petra* I will build (*oikodomēsō*) my church (*ekklēsian*, accusative of *ekklēsia*)." Much ink has been spilled about the meaning of the name pun, particularly in jousts between Protestants and Roman Catholics. In Aristotle's fourth-century Attic Greek, *petra* ("bedrock") was technically a different word than *petros* (stone, sometimes handheld). Some argue Jesus is contrasting Peter's unstable rolling-stone nature to the bedrock-like faith of the church, but the two words were likely synonyms for bedrock in the *koine* Greek of Jesus' time, *petros* grammatically masculine and *petra* grammatically feminine, with *lithos* serving for smaller stones.

---

9. Witherington, *Invitation to the New Testament,* 311.

I believe this passage offers a different, deeper set of puns that go beyond the choice of a new name. You can see the word Jesus chooses for "build" begins with a form of the Greek *oikos*, and combines it with a form of the verb "to build." The verb might be translated more literally as "I will build the *oikos*." However (in contrast to Aristotle), Jesus' *oikos*, the household in this new sort of kingdom, will be an *ekklēsia*.

You may have wondered why we use a word like "church" for gatherings of Jesus' disciples. Why did these Jewish followers of Messiah not retain the word "synagogue," a transliteration of the Greek for "together gathering?"[10]

The distinctive word for "churches" exists because the New Testament uses a Greek word different from synagogue for groups of Jesus' followers. Some seminaries still honor this distinction by teaching courses on "ecclesiology," the nature and function of the church. When the New Testament authors used "*ekklēsia*" of their gatherings, the word was already in use throughout the Empire. It refers to the political structure of free Hellenistic cities, like those in the Decapolis near Galilee. These cities had home rule that followed local custom, and thus they conformed to the traditional Aristotelian *polis* political structure. As we have seen, this involved a group of *oikos* households that were in no way internally democratic, each dominated by a *paterfamilias*. This potentially tyrannical institution was paired to the egalitarian *polis* of free *paterfamilias* citizens, marked by mutual respect, deference, and thoughtful persuasion.

The egalitarian assembly of the *polis* leaders in Roman free cities was called the *ekklēsia*. Just as Matthew's household code had inverted the received political institutions of Rome and Greece, the very naming of the church speaks of the same initiative. Jesus' *oikos* is being built as an *ekklēsia;* every person in Jesus' church—male, female, adult, child, slave—should be considered the equivalent of a *paterfamilias*.

---

10. The English word "church" derives from *kyrios*, "Lord," but gatherings of Christians have never called their meetings "Lords"! So we will have to dig back into the original language to pursue the answer.

By the way, some have argued this section of Matthew (in chapter 16), by using the word *ekklēsia,* is referencing an advanced level of church organization that only existed long after Matthew's lifetime. If that were so, this gospel must not be the work of the apostle (or any apostle). I believe I've just given a compelling alternative explanation of Matthew's use of this word.

Failure, mercy, ministry

Following Peter's great confession of faith, the gospels give witness to his rich but bumpy apprenticeship and ministry. Though enthusiastic and eager, he suffers a debilitating failure and loss of face during Jesus' arrest and trial. Immediately after an evening of great bravado, he runs away at the arrest, then sheepishly tags along as a voyeur at the trial. Found out, he brings down curses on himself to emphasize he has no interest whatsoever in the convicts' future. (Some translators suggest his curses may have been aimed at Jesus, not himself.) Ashamed and profoundly shaken, he slinked off and "wept bitterly."[11]

Though an early witness of the empty grave—his enthusiasm reappears in his mad dash to the site—Peter seems to carry from it an unresolved burden of shame and failure. He takes a band of the disciples and leaves Jerusalem to return to fishing. John ultimately records a heart-breaking conversation on the shore of the familiar Sea of Galilee in which Peter is personally reinstated to the group—commissioned three times, echoing his three denials. If Peter knew what it was to give up comfort and live constantly in the shadow of persecution, he also knew what it was to fail under persecution and live with profound regret. This experience no doubt shapes his later writing to the churches.

Paul reports when he met (mid-first-century) with Peter, James, and John, they all agreed Paul's primary calling would be toward Gentiles, Peter's toward Jews. But this should not obscure Peter's earlier pivotal role in the expansion of the Jesus movement

11. Luke 22:62; Matt 26:75.

to non-Jews, nor his later ministry through 1 Peter. Peter emerges in the opening chapters of Acts as the trailblazer of the early Jerusalem-centered Jesus movement. Peter leads in both public witness and internal church discipline. He is arrested twice in quick succession. Then comes a widespread persecution that disperses most believers to outlying areas; the apostles, led by Peter, stay to face the storm. Peter and John are then called to Samaria, where the events of Pentecost are now repeated at their hands *among Samaritans.* The Jerusalem persecution dies down, and Peter adopts an itinerant ministry reminiscent of Jesus'. He walks to the more-Hellenized Mediterranean coast, passing through Lydda to the coastal city of Joppa. He stays there "for some time" with a believing tanner—sharing in his chronic ritual uncleanness due to contact with dead animals.

Note the "Jonah" theme in Peter's life. Jesus had pointedly called him "Simon, son of Jonah." Like Jonah, Peter runs in the wrong direction at a crucial moment for public witness, during Jesus' trial. And now Peter stands in Joppa, the city from which Jonah tried to evade his calling. Peter is about to face a decisive moment in the redemption of his name. He receives a vision indicating he has misunderstood the intent of Jewish purification laws, which had the effect of barring Gentiles from his ministry. After the vision he immediately is confronted with Gentile emissaries of a Roman centurion stationed in the Hellenized provincial capital, Caesarea Maritima. Peter takes them in as house guests (more ritual impurity!), and within two days the events of Pentecost are again repeated, this time in Caesarea among *Gentiles.*

The Jewish believers around Peter are dumbfounded, but Peter does not miss a beat. "Can anyone now withhold baptism?" This is a remarkable question, in that Gentile converts to Judaism would normally first offer a sacrifice and be circumcised before being accepted as proselytes through baptism. The obvious answer to Peter's question would be "Yes, we should withhold baptism! They are not circumcised! They have not made sacrifices!" And for Peter to suggest this course of action in the presence of a centurion and his Gentile friends in the Roman provincial capital is especially daring. Jews had special standing in Roman law, legal privileges not accorded to the other "eastern religions." By distancing the Jesus movement from Jewish initiation rites, Peter calls into question his own movement's legal protections, protections that were indeed withdrawn by 96 CE, if not sooner.

Yet the Gentiles are baptized, and now Peter lodges with *them* for several days—even more ritual impurity! This is the surprising genesis of the presence of Gentiles as equals among the followers of Jesus.

Peter returns to Jerusalem, where he is eventually arrested a third time under what must have been terrifying circumstances. Herod Agrippa has killed James, and now has arrested Peter *at the Passover festival.* This striking parallel to Jesus' arrest must have left Peter anticipating the worst. Instead, there is a miraculous escape. He then "went to another place," and was apparently involved in the development of the Christian church in Syrian Antioch and elsewhere in Asia Minor.[12] This Antioch is the former Seleucid capital, and the Roman Empire's third-largest city; the church there sponsored Paul's missionary trips. While there, Peter briefly vacillates, in deference to James, on the full ceremonial inclusion of Gentiles into the church at Antioch: he withdraws from common meals with them, over concerns about ritual impurity. Paul points out the inconsistency of his behavior, and Peter is once again regretting a lapse in judgment. The next thing we hear of Peter is his opening statement at the first Jerusalem church council, in which he defends the details of Paul and Barnabas's ministry to Gentiles.

Peter and his wife likely continued an itinerant ministry.[13] This may have included northern Asia Minor, to which 1 Peter is addressed, perhaps among churches founded by returnees from his Pentecost sermon recorded in Acts 2. Late first-century tradition places him eventually in Rome. The text of 1 Peter 5:13 seems to be consistent with this tradition, using the "Babylon" euphemism for "Rome" that became common among Jewish writers. The suggestions that he founded the Roman church or was its first bishop

12. First Peter, 1 Clement 5:1–4, and Ignatius's *Romans* 4:3 suggest as much.
13. See 1 Corinthians 9:5.

appear to come along a few generations later. If they are true, one wonders why there is no mention of Peter among the many greetings in Paul's letter to Rome (about 58 CE), or in Acts' account of Paul's time in Rome (around 60 CE).

Tradition[14] and several New Testament intimations suggest the Gospel of Mark reflects Peter's teaching and witness to Jesus' life, written (probably in Rome) as a collaboration between the apostle and the "my son Mark" mentioned at the end of 1 Peter. Peter was likely martyred in Rome by Nero (suggested, for example, in Clement of Rome's letter to the Corinthians, 96 CE), probably in 64 CE, several months after the great Roman fire, perhaps as part of the festivities celebrating the tenth anniversary of Nero's assumption of power. It is likely that Paul's martyrdom happened at about the same time.

Thus Peter's life as an apostle was, from the beginning, an exercise in the loss of comforts, the reality of persecutions, the heartache of failure under pressure, and the delight of seeing new life emerge in the most unlikely of places. These themes are evident in his message of encouragement to marginalized believers: 1 Peter.

Peter's wit

At the beginning of chapter 3, when we were first considering the issue of Peter's knowledge of Greek ideas, I suggested the possibility of wryly misquoting a widely-known phrase as a way of making an emphatic point. I mentioned "life, liberty, and the pursuit of chocolate." In the next chapter I will suggest Peter may sometimes use the same approach to comment on the Aristotelian household code. I want to close this chapter with a brief survey of the first-century literary landscape that used similar conventions, before moving on to a close reading of Aristotle and Peter in the next chapter. I'm doing this to show that it would not be a big surprise to Peter's readers if he were to subvert Aristotle by selectively

14. Papias, Irenaeus, and Clement of Alexandria are cited by Eusebius. He cites Tertullian, Gaius, and Dionysius of Corinth regarding Peter's death during Nero's persecution in Rome.

misquoting him, inverting his ideas, or replacing a familiar Aristotelian phrase with a new one.

Unfortunately for our purposes, scholars of these conventions in the first century CE usually translate the name of the genre as "Roman satire." When I suggest to a friend that Peter might occasionally engage in "satire," they often withdraw in something akin to disgust. In their view, "satire" is the domain of coarse, cynical, mean-spirited people; how could Holy Scripture include *satire*?

I think it is well to acknowledge academics sometimes use words in a precise, technical sense that is not common in everyday speech. For example, referring to something in literature as "myth" does not mean it is untrue, as that word might mean in everyday usage; "myth" just means something is a coherent belief structure. If we are going to draw on the scholarship about Roman writing in the first century, we need to adopt a similar, technical meaning for the word "satire."

In the *Encyclopaedia Britannica*,[15] Robert C. Elliott introduces satire as an

> artistic form, chiefly literary and dramatic, in which human or individual vices, follies, abuses, or shortcomings are held up to censure by means of ridicule, derision, burlesque, irony, parody, caricature, or other methods, sometimes with an intent to inspire social reform . . . It is one of the most heavily worked literary designations and one of the most imprecise.

If we can allow a broad technical definition of satire, parts of Peter's letter may qualify. In fact, it may be the failure to read parts of 1 Peter as a parody of Aristotle that has left interpreters with few good options. Satire, understood in this sense, was a recognized literary genre in first-century Roman culture, a genre experiencing growth and development. It was often used to bring social injustices to light, and eventually came in several—at least four—flavors.

Menippean satire (after Menippus of Gadara, third century BCE) combined prose and verse (which, we will see, Peter also

---

15. Elliott, *Satire*.

does), and leaned toward parody (which I believe Peter also occasionally does, sometimes by juxtaposition). This form of Roman writing tends to address general attitudes, not attack individuals. *Horatian* satire (after the Roman Horace of the first century BCE) leaned toward gentle wit or exaggeration to criticize social folly or common human foibles and misperceptions. In both cases, one thinks of Will Rogers or Garrison Keillor or perhaps Mark Twain as modern practitioners of these sorts of satire. *Juvenalian* satire (after Juvenal, around the turn of the first century CE) developed some Horatian instincts into abrasive attacks on persons and social institutions, and labeled things evil as frequently as folly. This style is not a stranger to rage and polarization. Some have mentioned Voltaire, Orwell, and Huxley as modern inheritors of this tradition. *Verse* satire is written in the heroic meter of epic poetry—dactylic hexameter, lines of six feet, each composed of dactyls (one long/stressed syllable + two short/unstressed syllables). Many mark the first full-fledged Roman satirist as Gaius Lucilius, whose life spanned most of the first century BCE and whose work only exists as fragments of verse. It is clear Peter does not engage in either Juvenalian or Verse satire.

If Peter does indeed occasionally invoke the tradition of some Roman satire, the timing of his letter at mid-century would be consistent with the sort of gentle parody that was well known in that period. I only want to suggest that parody, juxtaposition, irony, and the humor of "deleting the expected" were all familiar literary forms of expression in the first century CE. We should not be surprised if Peter employed some of these conventions. They would rest easily within the style of *koine* Greek that scholars observe in 1 Peter—so-called "Asiatic Greek" and "Asiatic rhetoric"— which tended toward elongated sentences rich in hyperbole and metaphor.[16]

---

16. E.g., Witherington, *Invitation to the New Testament*, 307.

5

The *Oikos* of God

THE WRITERS OF THE New Testament were holding together a movement mainstream Gentiles harassed as an atheistic, unpatriotic, impious, eccentric cult.

Christians did not accept ancestral pagan cults. This could create significant strife within their marriages and extended families, because it directly challenged the duties and rights of the *paterfamilias*.[1] It caused strife beyond the extended family as well, because the empire had been cast as one enormous household headed by Caesar. Challenging the traditions of the household was viewed as a threat to the stability of the state.[2]

Christians also proclaimed a new Lord who bore the titles reserved for the emperor, and this "Lord" was a criminal whom Romans had *crucified*, a means of capital punishment so shameful it was reserved for non-citizens and only spoken of indirectly. Christians opposed participation in the imperial cult—they would not offer sacrifices at the emperor's image, and would not accept Caligula's divinizing statues, Nero's claims to divinity or Domitian's self-proclaimed title "Lord and God." This failure to participate in the imperial cult was taken as a further rejection of the emperor's right to rule. As if that were not enough, Christians went on to ethically

1. E.g., Fiorenza, *1 Peter,* 56.
2. E.g., ibid., 64.

and morally critique public cultural and political practices, whereas many of their fellow citizens seemed to go about their public life as if it were completely unconnected to their religious observance.

Christians did not practice astrology, use amulets or charms or incantations, or seek special favors and messages from the gods. Christians did not participate in community sacrifices to deities (or ritual sexuality), even when community sacrifices were a part of the routine mealtime social events associated with Asia Minor's many professional and industrial guilds, meant to build business and social connections.[3] In our day this would probably be something like shunning repeated invitations to join the Rotary Club.

Christians were, predictably, accused of an abundance of mischief, including cannibalism, incest, and the disruption of trade. And unlike the many achievement-driven, secretive-yet-inclusive "mystery cults" that offered fellowship, afterlife, and ecstatic spiritual/carnal experiences, the Christian social gatherings laid out expectations that their members would pursue ongoing personal, moral, and civic renovation. In repudiating the mystery cults and professional guilds, the Christians appeared to be deliberately, personally repudiating their social responsibilities and civic loyalties.[4]

The contempt experienced by these believers is all the more dangerous because they no longer lived under the limited legal protection offered to Jews by the empire. First Peter 4:16 signals they were viewed no longer as a Jewish sect, but as *Xhristianos,* "Christ-toadies," an epithet believers first encountered at Antioch and which was now spreading throughout the empire. We can get a feel for the hostility their distinctive behavior generated by reviewing an excerpt from the Roman historian and senator Tacitus's *Annals* (into which I've placed a few parenthetical explanations), describing attitudes in Rome at just about the time Peter would have been there writing 1 Peter:

---

3. These trade associations are richly documented by Elliott, *A Home for the Homeless,* 70. It appears at least some of them also adopted *oikos* as a self-description. (Ibid., 180)

4. Ibid., 78.

> Nero fastened the guilt (for the great fire in Rome) and inflicted the most exquisite tortures on a class hated for their abominations, called "Christians" by the populace. Christus, from whom the name had its origin, suffered the extreme penalty (note the euphemism for "crucifixion") during the reign of Tiberius at the hands of one of our procurators, Pontius Pilatus, and a most mischievous superstition, thus checked for the moment, again broke out not only in Judea, the first source of the evil, but even in Rome, where all things hideous and shameful from every part of the world find their center and become popular. Accordingly, an arrest was first made of all who pleaded guilty; then, upon their information, an immense multitude was convicted, not so much of the crime of firing the city, as of hatred against humankind.[5]

There you have it. Christians are abominable, worthy of hatred, mischievous, evil, hideous, shameful, haters of humankind. No longer protected as a movement within the licensed religion of Judaism, they are open to legal persecution;[6] Christianity was a *superstitio*, an illegal religion that threatened the social order. Christians were subject to daily social pressure and, in principle, could be persecuted, have their property seized, be prosecuted for offending the gods, and in the extreme case, be executed.[7]

The leaders of this movement held it together, in part, by writing letters—letters that travelled long distances, were subject to being stolen and read by hostile parties, and could have served as evidence against the recipients and authors. Yet the writers were establishing a new social framework that, under Jesus' own teaching, must look radically different from the surrounding secular culture.

---

5. Tacitus, *Annals*, 15.44. Fiorenza notes: "In many non-Christian first-century sources, the names "Christ" and "Christian" seem to be associated with public disorder." (*1 Peter*, 39)

6. True, though in 1 Peter the verbs seem to indicate (2:12, 3:3, 3:16, 4:14) verbal rather than legal (or physical) abuse. See Elliott, *A Home for the Homeless*, 80.

7. Witherington, *Invitation to the New Testament*, 50.

In this context, it seems reasonable the New Testament writers may sometimes have been indirect or subtle when they encouraged believers to resist some of the culture's norms. One thinks of a clever Eastern European dissident in the Soviet era, communicating via *samizdat* leaflets that appeared to be "nothing new," just the Party line. They communicated by the way they misquoted, truncated, or juxtaposed elements from the mainstream orthodoxy. We saw this sort of subtle approach earlier in Matthew 19 and Mark 10, where the authors did not say, in so many words, "those official household codes get everything completely backwards and upside-down!" But that was indeed the author's message.

This chapter considers the possibility that 1 Peter's household code is doing the same thing. Unfortunately, the author's subtlety, intended to protect their flock from the casual hostile reader of his day, also makes things difficult for readers like us, centuries away in a very different culture. No wonder so many commentators think Peter is just repeating Rome's party line! We will try to span this divide of time and culture by placing Peter's code alongside Aristotle's, and giving each a close reading.

Greek household-code ideas in a Roman world

We have seen that Aristotle's fourth-century BCE code survived and was substantially binding on first-century CE culture. Arius Didymus's influence, and the testimony of Seneca the Younger over a century later, make this clear.[8] But we should note the Roman imperial context is not identical to Aristotle's Greek city-state context. By Peter's day, the *paterfamilias* is considered the embodiment of the animating spirit of his clan (the *genius* of the *gens*). The *paterfamilias* is responsible for ensuring the extended household honors its *genius* cult—he was owed this duty from his family. He is responsible to maintain the family's obligations toward the local protecting spirit-guardians (*lares,* placed at the table for meals and significant events) and the household deities (*penates*). He must

8. Krentz, "Order in the 'House' of God," 285; Balch, *Let Wives be Submissive,* 39–44.

sustain culturally-acceptable moral standards within the extended household. If he or members of the extended family resist joining in or leading the pagan family cults—that is, if they advocate *atheism*—an enforcer representing the state might become involved.

In addition to the *paterfamilias's* moral and priestly duties, he was chief executive officer of an estate-based enterprise. All property acquired by his adult children and slaves was the property of the *paterfamilias* until his death. He could order a woman in the extended family to denounce a child or sell it into slavery or abandon a newly born child to die (and he was, in principal, required to do so if the infant were "obviously deformed"[9]).

Only a Roman citizen could hold the status of *paterfamilias.* The authority of the *paterfamilias* over his daughters, even married daughters, generally continued until his death, his release of the daughter's property to her husband's *paterfamilias*, his emancipation of the daughter (granting the right to initiate independent legal actions, under an appointed male guardian), or the death of the daughter's husband. At the time of a *paterfamilias's* death, male children living independently acquire the status of *paterfamilias* in their own households; any earlier emancipation of male children amounted to disinheritance.

The place of women in the Roman Imperial era had become a bit less desperate than in fifth-century-BC Athens. Women attained some limited property rights, though women outside the Imperial court never gained political or voting rights.[10] Marriage, which was generally a property relationship pursued for financial reasons,[11] took several forms, all of which left the woman in a position resembling that of a grown child within a family.[12] The bride's property, minus a dowry to be returned in the event of divorce,

---

9. *Lex Duodecim Tabularum* (The Twelve Tables, the earliest written Roman code of law and earliest surviving Roman literature), Table IV, Law 1. See Cicero, *de Legibus*, 3, 8, 19.

10. Koester, *Introduction to the New Testament*, 63–64.

11. "Marriage . . . had little relation to love . . . Tenderness and warmth between blood relatives was not considered important." Ibid., 65.

12. Krentz, "Order in the 'House' of God," 284.

would typically remain with her *paterfamilias*. (This was already the norm by the beginning of the empire.) The daughter might instead be wed *in manu*: her current and future property was transferred to her husband's *paterfamilias*.[13] In either case, both *patres familia* must agree to the marriage and the dowry (and, from 100 BCE on, both the bride and groom must also agree to be married). Such were the general terms of marriage for Romans; in some eastern portions of the empire, customs were more harsh toward the woman.

Bride and groom would have the right to divorce by simply separating, witnessed by a letter or by several persons. If a man divorced his wife, the dowry would return to the wife's *paterfamilias*. If the wife's *paterfamilias* had died, the dowry passed back to the wife, giving her some cushion on which to land. However, if the divorce involved a wife's misdeeds (the law did not admit the possibility of misdeeds by the male unless someone's wife was involved) or if there were children (who were considered the property of the man), the dowry was split between wife and husband. Again, in the east, males sometimes had more advantages; sometimes women had no option to divorce, with limited property rights in the event their husbands left them.

As Augustus expanded imperial authority over some of the *paterfamilias*'s duties, one change was a slave might in principle appeal to a *censor* in the event of very harsh treatment. This may have been an accommodation to maintain order after three slave revolts around 100 BCE. However, we have no record that such an appeal by a slave to a *censor* was ever filed, let alone filed successfully. Slaves were subject to corporal punishment, and in some eras the testimony of a slave was only admissible in court if it had been extracted by torture.[14] Slaves had a corresponding obligation to protect their master, to an extravagant degree: The *senatus con-*

---

13. There was also the option of a *usus*, "common law" arrangement, in which one year's cohabitation brought the woman under the man's authority, unless she left for three nights. This offers the woman some distance from her *paterfamilias* and her husband's authority.

14. Wiedemann, *Greek and Roman Slavery*, 167.

sultum Silanianum (10 CE) requires all slaves under the same roof at the time of a master's murder must be tortured and killed for their laxity in protecting him.

The slave's hope of eventually buying one's own freedom was one method for maintaining compliance among slaves. Slaves—especially skilled household slaves who served as physicians or teachers—could in principle take on employment or gradually save up enough money from their personal allowance to pay for their *manumission*. In practice, masters had control over how slaves used their time and set not only the allowance pay rates but also the manumission price. Masters were able to control manumission so it served their own ends. Young, productive slaves would have difficulty saving up enough to buy manumission; as slaves aged and lost productivity, they might eventually save up the manumission fee. From this fee the master could then buy a new, younger, more productive slave. In effect, the personal allowances of aging slaves could be used as a finance mechanism for their own replacement, at no additional cost to the master. If the slave's savings never amounted to enough to purchase freedom, those savings (and all the slave's other possessions) would revert to the master upon the slave's death.

Regarding children and parenting, we know the exposure of infants (infanticide by neglect) was widespread and often accepted as inevitable, even for viable and legitimate children.[15] Infanticide helped concentrate inheritances, and restrict to slaves the exertion of physical labor. Many sources indicate children were trained to absolutely and immediately obey, and failure to do so brought beatings for certain and the possibility of exile and disinheritance. To train children properly away from any tendency to disobey, the empire offered professional child-beaters. The beatings continued in school, as fear of beating was thought to be an excellent motivator of learning and morality. Since the learning consisted largely of rote memorization, one wonders about the emotional health of children who did not have a good natural capacity for memory.

15. See, e.g., Harris, "Child-Exposure in the Roman Empire."

When not being beaten, the sources we have suggest child-rape was common. Some scholars have argued sex with wives was an infrequent duty required of *patres familia* by the obligations of inheritance, but that child-rape was the normal male path of sexual gratification. This appears to have sometimes been condoned by the children's parents, who collected a fee.[16] Beginning with Tiberius (ruling 14–37 CE, coming to power in his mid-50s), sexual indulgence with children was particularly notorious in the imperial court. By 26 CE, Tiberius had deserted Rome to live on Capri, surrounded by pornography and, so the sources indicate, addicted to every sort of self-gratification with children of all ages. Caligula, Nero, and Domitian are reported to have continued in this tradition of imperial depravity.[17]

When they tired of children, *patres familia* could turn to sex slaves. Though slavery was rationalized as necessary to agricultural production, roughly 40 percent of the empire's slaves were not in the bread-bowl provinces but in Italy, where slaves made up perhaps one-third of the population. Many were forced to function as sex slaves, not only to their masters and mistresses, but to anyone to whom the master granted permission, such as house guests.[18]

Underlying these husband-wife, master-slave, and father-child relationships lay a legal theory. Romans, like Aristotle, emphasized that justice is based on equality (that is, treating equals equally). Thus justice can exist only among those who are friends on the basis of equality—who are equals. There is no justice in the equal treatment of those who are fundamentally not equal. Males

16 Williams, *Roman Homosexuality*; Brownmiller, *Against Our Will*.

17. Some have suggested our sources in these Imperial matters should perhaps be discounted, as if they are the equivalent of tabloid journalism. But it is undeniable that non-consensual child sex was common, especially among the landed male aristocracy. Discussing the financially-dominated motives for marriage and the low expectations for warmth among blood relatives, Koester (*Introduction*, 65) comments: "A husband might have his most intimate personal relationship with a young slave, boy or girl, whom he kept as a concubine and page. The story of the boy Antinoos, who was the pet of the emperor Hadrian, is typical."

18. Vinson et al., *1 and 2 Peter, Jude*, 121.

and females, or masters and slaves, or fathers and children, as unequals, must be treated differently in order to maintain justice. This probably explains the tendency toward lax treatment of the *paterfamilias* when he abuses those in the underclasses—which is to say, when he abuses anyone.

Peter characterizes this entire cultural matrix as "futile ways inherited from your ancestors"[19] from which believers have been ransomed by a spiritual manumission from slavery: "You have already spent enough time in doing what the Gentiles like to do, living in licentiousness, passions, drunkenness, revels, carousing, and lawless idolatry. They are surprised that you no longer join them in the same excesses of dissipation, and so they blaspheme."[20]

Making sense of the New Testament Household Codes

Before we dive into the texts of Peter's and Aristotle's codes, let us reflect for a moment on this *paterfamilias-oikos* economic-political arrangement—on its deep brutality. It is difficult for anyone to enter into any role in this system while retaining one's humanity. The nature of these arrangements is to degrade, humiliate, intimidate, and exploit. In the end, the person ostensibly at the top of the pyramid, the *paterfamilias,* becomes the most animallike and subhuman creature in the system.

Now bring these reflections alongside of our review, in chapter 1, of the current state of interpretation of the New Testament household codes. Those interpretations propose the apostles endorsed Roman culture's household codes in the interest of maintaining church order, or hoping to promote evangelism, or out of fear of reprisals, or under the belief that the Roman order actually allowed for mutual respect and dignity. Is it really likely that Jesus' disciples would not have challenged such a brutal system?

To begin answering that question, I think a distinction among the New Testament codes may be helpful. All but Peter's—Ephesians,

19. 1 Pet 1:18.
20. Ibid., 4:3–4.

Colossians, and the material that is somewhat related to household codes in 1 Timothy and Titus—are written to three particular localities—Ephesus, Crete (probably Gortyna and Knossos), and Colossae. These code-related passages are very brief, and only two—in Ephesians and Colossians, which are nearly identical—actually follow the form of Aristotelian codes; the others may be more properly thought of as discussions of church leadership positions. All four letters probably address a relatively small number of believers within each of those localities. The letters themselves suggest there are special features of these local cultures which the authors have taken into account. We must therefore be cautious when interpreting those codes, because there may be unique situations and personalities in play, now invisible to us.

Colossae has never been excavated, so many details remain a mystery. Philemon is addressed to the same community, and it is not entirely clear how one should reconcile the messages of the two letters—one containing an extremely brief code that resembles parts of Aristotle, the other explaining that Paul has been violating the fugitive slave law in order to shelter a Colossian slave. Regarding Ephesus, some have argued some practices of the cult of Artemis—males were apparently presumed to have brought sin into the world, and were submitted to cultic rebirth through a stone vaginal sculpture—provide a context that significantly reframes the words of the code materials in Ephesians and 1 Timothy. But we do not have clear evidence these cult practices existed as early as the first century CE.

It may also be that, when an author addresses one small local group of followers about a particular situation, the text may often aim to make the best of a bad situation, rather than focusing on long-term change. Imagine the difference between Dr. Martin Luther King addressing the 1963 March on Washington, and Dr. King discussing tactics with a small group of organizers before a particular civil protest. In one case, the whole culture comes under review; in the other, the focus will be on living well and peacefully within many of the structures that are in place. Surely when Dr. King told demonstrators in Selma to not resist violence, to meet unjust behavior with submission and kindness, he was not advocating acceptance of or submission to the system of segregation. The tactic of non-resistance was in service to an overall strategy of dismantling the entire system.

In general, it seems best to interpret the more obscure and locally-focused Bible passages in light of less-obscure, widely-addressed passages, like 1 Peter. First Peter is "the only New Testament document that systematically addresses the issue of Christians . . . being resident aliens within the macrostructures of the larger society,"[21] and "no document in the New Testament offers a more rich and developed understanding of Christian suffering and how it is like Christ's suffering."[22] So it will be especially important to understand the teaching of 1 Peter—an encyclical written to many groups in a variety of circumstances—concerning the *paterfamilias-oikos* household structure. I intend to show in 1 Peter the author is casting off the Aristotelian household code.

Peter's epistle: Opening statement

Peter's code is central to his book. His code is actually split into two sections, I believe, with commentary before, between, and after. I do not mean to suggest everything in the letter must be read through the lens of the household code material, but the code is central enough that we might expect to see some themes carried throughout the book that are relevant to understanding Peter's attitude toward Aristotle. With that in mind, let me briefly summarize some of the ideas in Peter's first paragraphs, before we consider his formal introduction to his household code.

You can tell what sort of letter this will be from the opening greeting. Peter addresses his flock as "God's selected ones, strangers in the world, exiles of the *diaspora*." All three titles would call up deep associations. "Selected" is a reference to the covenants with God's chosen people throughout history; "strangers" is a reference to the Hebrew Scripture's word for resident aliens; "*diaspora*" is the

21. Witherington, *Invitation to the New Testament,* 298.

22. Ibid., 320.

Jewish reference for God's people dispersed, scattered geographically and culturally among the Gentiles, as in exile. Peter is writing to believers who are dear to God but dispersed in unfriendly, bewildering territory. Throughout the letter's introduction he will invoke images from the history of Israel, contrasting the community among believers to their uneasy life in a hostile culture.[23]

A typical first-century epistle would follow this brief salutation with a prayer or blessing. The blessing usually introduces the themes of the letter. Thus by verse 3 Peter is directing praise to God that the believers have been "given new birth into a living hope . . . and an unfading inheritance . . . even if you have had to briefly suffer various sorrows." Those two ideas—present sufferings, eventual inheritance—run through the blessing section. Peter identifies them in the life of Jesus, the lives of the prophets, and the lives of Peter and his flock. These themes are not unrelated to the household code to follow: believers are being ostracized because they reject so much of mainstream culture. Peter epitomizes this tension by saying all believers—slave, free, male, female—are *inheritors*, equal coinheriting children, in the countercultural *oikos* which is the church, the "household of God."

After the blessing, a typical letter often includes a report on the writer's circumstances. By deleting this, Peter signals this letter will be about his *recipients'* circumstances. It may say something about Peter's character that he does not attract attention to himself, despite his prominent position in the church, living in the belly of the beast and facing impending persecution and martyrdom. Instead he moves on to the first element in the body of a typical first-century letter: a request (or exhortation). This is usually followed by the body of the letter, which often begins with a thesis statement. Peter's

---

23. Some adventurous commentators have argued the alien/sojourner titles indicate this letter is addressed to Roman colonists in the provinces. This seems unlikely. Acts 7 uses these words twice to refer to the heritage of God's people in unfriendly places, as does Hebrews 11:9. Philo does as well (*The Cherubim,* 120–21.) The Qumran community had a similar concept, but referred to themselves as *exiles,* emphasizing their withdrawal from the surrounding culture, whereas Peter speaks of "diaspora," "aliens," and "sojourners"—all indicating the navigation of life *in* society rather than apart from it.

request/exhortation (1:13—2:8) is actually a string of exhortations, leading up to what I take to be his thesis statement (2:9).

The exhortation begins with an appeal to discipline your thinking (1:13), redirect your desires (1:14), and renovate your behavior (1:15–16). You can see Peter is playing with the three-theme soul (thought, desire, and behavior) the Greek philosophers had proposed. Both Plato and Aristotle made thinking/intellect/reason primary over desire and behavior. Aristotle defines humans as *rational* animals, then goes on to argue some humans (free men) have more reason than others, and free men must therefore dominate.

Peter, by contrast, simply places thought, desire, and action alongside each other, interdependent with each other. By doing this, Peter has undercut the anthropology, the theory of the human person, that supports Aristotle's household code. Aristotle's foundation is replaced with the belief that, to the extent church members differ in their endowments in these three areas, that difference should be *valued* as a healthy diversity of gifts, all of which are given to serve the common good. (First Peter 4:10–11 makes this explicit, and calls believers *oikonomoi,* administering these gifts as "*oikos* stewards.") At the same time, this new anthropology implies "conversion" is a much richer experience than just accepting some new thoughts or beliefs. Desires become rightly oriented, behavior is redirected, and thinking is renovated, each element complementing and reinforcing the others.

There follows a long development (leading up to the household code) of the ways in which acting/behaving is now to be different during the church's exile. Behavior should no longer conform to the "futile ways" that were inherited from ancestors (1:18) because believers have been *set free* from that futility; the verb indicates a manumission from joint slavery into joint free status. Behavior is instead marked by deep mutual love (1:22) in this new family into which they have been born, in which everyone is an equal inheritor. The content of this love is expounded (2:1–8): it is sincere and humble, as they are together built as living stones into a spiritual household (*oikos*). They are to be a spiritual priesthood offering *spiritual sacrifices* acceptable to God through Jesus

Christ, the cornerstone of the *oikos* who has been rejected by the mainstream. Here at 2:5, and again at 4:17, as bookends around his household code, Peter invokes the vision of the Christian community as an alternative *oikos*.

Surely at this point the hearers recalled the *pagan* sacrifices that formed the spiritual duties of the *paterfamilias*-priest. They likely also contrasted the deep mutual love and universal inheritance rights of this *oikos* with the atmosphere of the typical Roman *oikos*. They likely saw the contrast between the high behavioral expectations of the church and the low view of social and personal morality within the pagan mystery religions. And they perhaps again marveled that every person is functioning as an equal partner in this new *oikos*. Peter has been referring to the entire community of believers as if they are equals, a single entity; he does not address people according to their gender, property status, servitude, education, or any other marker. Unlike Aristotle's code, everyone receives the same message.

These themes will continue in a most remarkable way. At 2:9 we land at the thesis statement to which the entire letter might, in one way or another, be linked. But first let me note Peter is not advocating a program of self-improvement by the strength of one's own will. Throughout his introduction he has made references to God's mercy and initiative, the power that fuels the new life he envisions. As if to amplify this theme, he has woven in the three theological virtues—hope in the first paragraph, faith and hope in the second, and love in the third. The apostles did not come peddling a mystery cult of individual ecstasy, nor psychological adjustment, nor mere salvation of individual souls from a corrupt physical realm destined for destruction. They proclaimed the resurrection power of God loosed on the world, a new reality in which all things in creation would be made new, beginning with the church, God's new humanity, and extending to every principality and power.

Peter now introduces and develops his household code, which we will explore in parallel with the relevant sections of Aristotle's code.

The two codes

Ways of knowing: Introspection and revelation

1 Peter: 2–3

Aristotle, *Politics*

⁹But you are a chosen race, a royal priesthood, a holy nation, God's own people, in order that you may proclaim the mighty acts of him who called you out of darkness into his marvelous light.

¹⁰Once you were not a people,

but now you are God's people;

once you had not received mercy,

but now you have received mercy.

I.13: Here the very constitution of the soul has shown us the way; in it one part naturally rules, and the other is subject . . . :III.4: Again, the state, as composed of unlikes, may be compared to the living being: as the first elements into which a living being is resolved are soul and body, as soul is made up of rational principle and appetite, the family of husband and wife, property of master and slave, so of all these, as well as other dissimilar elements, the state is composed; and, therefore, . . .

As we have seen before, the basis of Aristotle's code is introspection. Look within yourself, and you see a body and a soul; look within your soul, and you again see two parts—rational and sensual/appetite. Look around you, and you'll see the same dualism popping up in other places. By projecting his perceived intrapersonal dualism out onto political culture, Aristotle can argue the state is composed of persons who are "unlikes," some more rational, some more sensual/appetitive. Recall that his conception of justice amounts to treating equally those things that are alike. Thus Aristotle has laid the groundwork for treating classes of persons unequally under the law.

Peter appeals to a different source than introspection. You can see in these paragraphs that Peter believes when a typical person looks honestly within, they will see a deeply conflicted person, often attracted to the things that are most destructive—most unsuitable as a basis for constructing the social order. And this is no less true of males than of females. So Peter appeals not to introspection, but revelation. He has strung together a number of scriptural quotations already in his introduction, and here in verse 9 he quotes (or alludes to) passages from Exodus, Isaiah, and Malachi. He reinforces this with the psalm-like short poem of verse 10, built on quotations from Hosea. What do these quotations collectively teach? The *common* nature of man, woman, slave, and free, and their common need to be brought from darkness to light and fashioned into a new sort of community. When they are, their life together is not grounded in any member's powers of reason or natural strength or physical cravings; theirs is not the kingly-priesthood of the *paterfamilias,* but rather the kingly-priesthood mercifully established at Sinai, consummated in the person of Jesus, and now embodied in the life of his *ekklēsia* community, the "spiritual house" (*oikos,* 2:9) in which the divine king resides.[24]

In fact, verse 9 uses Aristotle's categories to undermine Aristotle. As we saw in chapter 2, Aristotle argues that to understand any *thing,* we must come to terms with its essence/nature, and its *telos,* its ultimate purpose and direction. Verse 9 first states the *nature* of a Christian believer, which is essentially communal: you (using a plural pronoun) are a chosen race, a royal priesthood, a holy nation, God's own people (all collective nouns). Then comes the *telos:* in order that (*opōs)* you (again plural) may proclaim the mighty acts of him who called you out of darkness into his marvelous light.

In this new humanity, you cannot define the nature of a person, or the purpose for that person's life, by analyzing this one person's attributes—the extent of their rationality, or their property-ownership status, or their gender—and then setting these attributes in opposition to those of other persons. Instead, Peter's vision of Aristotle's "good life which must be pursued" involves coming out of darkness, coming into marvelous light, making proclamation, and doing it all as a group of equals. The rest of the letter explores how this vision can be pursued under difficult circumstances.

As Sylvanus reads this letter aloud to small gatherings scattered around northern Asia Minor, churches comprised of men and women, slaves and estate owners, artisans and laborers sitting

---

24. For a full exposition of the relationship between *basileion* and *oikia* in these passages, see Elliott, *A Home for the Homeless,* 169.

in a room, they are each being directly addressed by the Apostle. These are not lecture notes addressed only to the superior free men in the room. The gathered believers hear that they are one, single race (*genos*). They are all priests. They are one common nation/culture (*ethnos*). They are God's own people—literally "people for (God's own) possession," not for the possession of some by the others. As they have been called out of the darkness around them that would deny each of these teachings, they together proclaim the acts and excellences of this God who reveals and renovates.

Honorable aliens

[11]Beloved, I urge you as aliens and exiles to abstain from the desires of the flesh that wage war against the soul. [12]Conduct yourselves honorably among the Gentiles, so that, though they malign you as evildoers, they may see your honorable deeds and glorify God when he comes to judge.

III.4: Therefore the virtue of all the citizens cannot possibly be the same, any more than the excellence of the leader of a chorus is the same as that of the performer who stands by his side. I have said enough to show why the two kinds of virtue cannot be absolutely and always the same ... V.11: Again, the evil practices of the last and worst form of democracy are all found in tyrannies. Such are the power given to women in their families in the hope that they will inform against their husbands, and the license which is allowed to slaves in order that they may betray their masters; for slaves and women do not conspire against tyrants; and they are of course friendly to tyrannies and also to democracies, since under them they have a good time.

This section of 1 Peter begins with a paragraph break from the preceding thesis statement, signaled by the use of vocative address, much as Aristotle signals with a "therefore." Aristotle takes this opportunity to draw out the implications of his anthropology for political inequality. Recall Plato's concern that a non-aristocratic form of governance will devolve into tyranny. For Aristotle, it is essential that the egalitarian, democratic atmosphere of the *paterfamilias's polis* must be complemented by the autocratic/aristocratic rule of the *paterfamilias* within his own extended household *oikos*. Here Aristotle weaves together his own ideas with those of Plato: if the supremacy of the *paterfamilias* over the *oikos* were challenged, if women or slaves were regarded as the equals of free men, this would lead to tyranny in the *polis*. The *paterfamilias oikos* system is essential to the common good.

Yet Peter proceeds unfazed. He addresses the gathered church as one, and invokes love ("Beloved . . .), absent from Aristotle's analysis, as if to highlight the contrast.[25] His paragraph underscores the other contrasts between life in the church and life in the surrounding culture: believers are aliens and exiles, maligned as unpatriotic atheists who do not care about the common good, because they do not join in with the excesses of cult worship and do not affirm the principles behind the *paterfamilias oikos*. Yet they must seek to behave in ways that their neighbors will deem honorable. Even the word used for "aliens" highlights the contrast between church and culture: though they are *resident aliens* (*paroikos*) who do not share in the practices of the pagan households, literally "by-dwellers" who don't enjoy the full acceptance of the surrounding culture, they are also *God's household* (*oikos*).

Peter's agenda for believers is clearly a very tall order. Peter proposes some guidelines for public behavior by giving one short orienting paragraph (vv. 13–16), then one brief poem (v. 17), then a detailed household code.

---

25. It may be significant that here (and in the other group vocatives at 3:8 and 4:12) Peter uses the gender-inclusive "beloved" or *pantes*, "all of you," rather than the *adelphoi*, "brothers," that might be expected.

Justice and the state's authority

[13] For the Lord's sake accept the authority of every human institution, whether of the emperor as supreme, [14] or of governors, as sent by him to punish those who do wrong and to praise those who do right. [15]For it is God's will that by doing right you should silence the ignorance of the foolish. [16]As servants* of God, live as free people, yet do not use your freedom as a pretext for evil.

III.9: But a state exists for the sake of a good life, and not for the sake of life only: if life only were the object, slaves and brute animals might form a state, but they cannot, for they have no share in happiness or in a life of free choice . . . VII.3: For the actions of a ruler cannot really be honorable, unless he is as much superior to other men as a husband is to a wife, or a father to his children, or a master to his slaves. For that which can foresee by the exercise of mind is by nature intended to be lord and master, and that which can with its body give effect to such foresight is a subject, and by nature a slave . . . I.5: For that some should rule and others be ruled is a thing not only necessary, but expedient.

Peter begins with a paragraph on the nature and authority of the state, just as Aristotle relates the proper *oikos* to the proper *polis*. In these passages Aristotle argues that rule of one free *paterfamilias* by another *paterfamilias* would be improper; in the process he establishes that a government and economy would be dishonorable and unnatural, oriented merely toward nutrition and survival, and ultimately unworkable, if not built on the power hierarchy that subsumes women, slaves, and children beneath a *paterfamilias*.[26] Peter has been rejecting just this hierarchy, and now, by contrast to Aristotle, omits all mention of the *paterfamilias-oikos* system in his discussion of the proper nature of the state. He acknowledges there

26. Recall that Arius Didymus inserted the notion that the state could be thought of as a really big *oikos*. He retained Aristotle's vision of the proper household, and since the *oikos* has monarchical (parent-child, master-slave) and aristocratic (husband-wife) elements, the state need not be democratic, so long as it is not oriented toward personal gain for those in leadership. None of this really matters for our discussion here—Peter's criticisms of Aristotle apply equally to Arius Didymus.

is indeed a legitimate authority in systems of governance, *to the extent that* they reward right behavior and restrain wrong behavior. For this reason there is hope that, by doing what is right, the unfair criticism and harassment of the church might eventually fall silent.

This hope is not necessarily experienced immediately, and certainly not automatically, of course. Peter had just said those who do good must be prepared to experience exclusion and unfair treatment. Peter draws this paradox together in the last, remarkable sentence of this paragraph: the entire community is to live as not-enslaved persons (*eleutheroi*), while simultaneously living as slaves (*douloi*) of God. They are obliged to align their lives with the ways of God's *oikos,* not those of the surrounding culture. With respect to that culture, they have been freed. Yet this freedom is bound by the need to do right, and must not be twisted into an argument for *kakias*—wickedness, malice, hostility. Peter's household code will explore how to thread this needle.

Note that Peter has continued to address men, women, and slaves in common. He grounds civil authority not in a natural right to power, but in the exercise of justice. By "justice" he means impartially rewarding good behavior and punishing bad, without respect to the social standing of the plaintiff. This is a profound departure from the notion that justice consists of treating social equals equally and social inferiors differently.

As Sylvanus reads these sentences to the gathered faithful, we might imagine a ripple of acknowledgment across the room. Peter tells them all, including the slaves in the room, to live as *free* persons. This is precisely what Aristotle finds to be unnatural, immoral, and unworkable. Peter has just argued everyone in the room—men, women, slaves—should be thought of as having equal deliberative capacities. Each person has freedom from the obligation to do what is not right, even if the deed is ordered by a social superior.

We must consider one more nuance of Peter's paragraph. The first phrase, rendered literally, would be "*upotassō* to every human creature." The verb is often translated as "submit to" or "be subject to," though I will argue this is not a helpful translation. If we translate as "submit to," it's difficult to see how everyone could submit to *everyone*. Acknowledging this problem, translations that invoke "submit" often translate the word "creature" as "human institution," anticipating the paragraphs that follow. But "it is hard to find a clear example of this meaning outside the Bible, and it never means this in biblical usage. Peter is not talking about submission to institutions, but submission to people."[27] This phrase, "every person should mutually *upotassō* to every person," stands as the theme sentence that is then fleshed out by several cases—behavior toward government, behavior of slaves, behavior of wives and husbands. We must work out a good translation of this word, but I think we will be best served by doing that when we are discussing Peter's advice to slaves and wives, just a few pages from now.

Chiastic poem on honor and love

[17]Honor everyone.
> Love (*agapē*) the family of believers.
> Fear God.
Honor the emperor.

I've reported the next element of text, Peter's brief poem, without a parallel passage from Aristotle, because there is no parallel Aristotelian passage discussing love in the household!

In the second half of this verse, Peter has strategically misquoted Proverbs 24:21: "Fear the Lord and the king, and do not disobey either of them." If he had quoted *verbatim,* this verse would build to a climax: *Honor* everyone, *love* the fellowship, *be in awe of* God and emperor. Instead, Peter's poem ends with an anti-climax, reverting back to *honor* for the emperor. It is a chiasm—the first and last thoughts mirroring each other, the second and second-to-last thoughts mirroring—so that we should hear some poetic emphasis on the central section.

27. Clowney, *The Message of 1 Peter,* 105.

"Love" may be somewhat alien to Aristotle, but "honor" (*timos*) was not. Timocracy was Plato's highest-attainable form of government, and Roman culture was saturated with patronage systems built on an ideology of honor. Those higher on the social ladder granted financial support to their underlings. In return, the patronized were then responsible to follow their patrons in the street at designated times, blowing noise-makers and shouting out praise of the patron's generosity. Jesus created the comic image (Matthew 6) of a person who wants the honor of being a patron without actually being generous enough to support others; he is reduced to blowing his own trumpet when he makes a contribution.

Here Peter places honor in a larger context, and in the process he redefines honor. In the midst of an honor-obsessed culture, believers are being shamed—harassed, gossiped against, excluded. Should they respond by shaming others? Or perhaps they—especially the property-owning males—should double-down on imitating the surrounding culture, to earn its approval? No. Instead they should seek to honor everyone, and seek to maintain behavior that is exemplary *by God's standards,* as honor ultimately rests in God's approval.

In a satire by understatement, Peter encourages honor of (though not fear or awe of) the emperor, not because the emperor is divine, nor because he sits atop the patronage system, nor because he is the *paterfamilias* of *patres familias,* but because he is a person, and every person should be honored. The emperor goes on the last line of the poem. Peter's is an inverted hierarchy. And honor, for those in the community of faith, points toward (as the first/last element in a chiasm points toward the middle element) the love (*agape*) toward believers and *phobeomai*—profound respect—toward God one finds within the community. Peter's word for this community (*adelphotēs*) connotes a strong sense of unity. Proper honor is built upon and points toward reverence for God and love for all sorts of persons. The honor/*timos* itself is not a proper foundation for the social order.

On slavery

Opening address

¹⁸Slaves, accept the authority of your masters with all deference, not only those who are kind and gentle but also those who are harsh.

I.5: For . . . from the hour of their birth, some are marked out for subjection, others for rule . . . Where then there is such a difference as that between soul and body, or between men and animals . . . the lower sort are by nature slaves, and it is better for them as for all inferiors that they should be under the rule of a master . . . I.7: The master is not called a master because he has science, but because he is of a certain character, . . . I.13: The virtue of the ruler . . . being the virtue of the rational, and the other of the irrational part. Although the parts of the soul are present in all of them (male, female, child, slave), they are present in different degrees. For the slave has no deliberative faculty at all . . . I.6: Hence we see what is the nature and office of a slave; he who is by nature not his own but another's man, is by nature a slave; and he may be said to be another's man who, being a human being, is also a possession.

¹⁹For it is to your credit if, being aware of God, you endure pain while suffering unjustly.

VII.3: And therefore he who violates the law can never recover by any success, however great, what he has already lost in departing from virtue. For equals the honorable and the just consist in sharing alike, as is just and equal. But that the unequal should be given to equals, and the unlike to those who are like, is contrary to nature, and nothing which is contrary to nature is good.

On the right we have Aristotle's rationale, familiar by now, for slavery, followed by his also-familiar conception of justice—treating equals equally, unequals unequally.

The preliminaries over, Peter here begins his actual household code with another paragraph break marked by a vocative. It is important to see Peter has been changing the emphasis of the letter since 2:11. Having developed the basis for a distinctive common life *within* the community of believers, he then laid down a transition toward talking about the life of believers *outside* that community, developing several specific cases. After establishing the basis for a profoundly distinctive community of "exiles and alien sojourners," he turns to advise those who are enmeshed in long-term obligations to people who live by different standards. This change in topic is clear from the way Peter describes those to whom the governed, slaves, and wives are relating.

As Sylvanus continues to read this letter to gathered communities of faith, some of them meeting in the homes of estate-owners,[28] we might again imagine a rustle of recognition as Peter begins a household code by addressing *slaves*.[29] We have no surviving ancient literature *at all,* until the New Testament, that addresses slaves directly,[30] and it is obvious no self-respecting Roman household code would address slaves, but Peter has elevated slaves to the first place in his code. This was anticipated in the letter's thesis-statement verse, 2:9, which quotes liberally from Exodus, an account of the liberation of slaves. As Fred Craddock puts it, when chains fall off the spirit, that fact alone threatens the whole institution of slavery.[31]

In fact, Peter never gives instructions to slave owners, whereas slave owners are the *only* persons Aristotle addresses. What accounts for this difference? There is a simple explanation: *Peter expects that none of his church's members would own slaves.* This is an implication of Peter's introduction to the letter, and also the most straightforward explanation of this omission from his household code.[32]

28. Elliott argues the norm in these regions would have been non-urban household-based congregations. (*A Home for the Homeless,* e.g., 64)

29. Some commentaries have made much of the fact that 1 Peter here uses a word (*oiketēs*) that suggests slaves who are a part of households, rather than the broader term (*doulos*) that would also connote agricultural and mining work. But if Peter's aim is to write a critique of Aristotle's treatment of slavery in his household code, we should not make too much of a detail like this; his point would be the use of a word that is linguistically linked to "household," rather than to limit the teaching to slaves who serve within households.

30. Vinson et al., *1 & 2 Peter, Jude,* 118–19.

31. Craddock, *First and Second Peter and Jude,* 50.

32. Craddock (ibid., 49) suggests this possibility as a parallel to teaching elsewhere in the New Testament. Jesus instructs those forced to go a mile, sued

We cannot be certain these churches in northern Asia Minor had seen copies of Paul's various letters, though the author of 2 Peter indicates his readers had indeed read some of them. If these believers had seen Philemon, addressed to a town not far away, they would have been primed for Peter's rejection of slave-owning. In Philemon, Paul explains he has risked his own well-being by violating the fugitive slave laws. Then he shames a slave-owning Christian into granting manumission, and thus Roman citizenship, to the escaped slave that Paul has been harboring. Or perhaps 1 Timothy had come their way, in which (1:9–12) Paul lists slave-trading as the work of lawless, disobedient, godless, sinful, unholy, and profane persons, contrary to the sound teaching of the glorious gospel.

But in this section of his household code, Peter is addressing slaves owned by pagans who would be utterly unmoved by Christian opposition to slavery. So what is a believing slave, owned by a nonbeliever, to do? Peter evidently believes slaves are capable of deliberation and self-direction. He indicates they can tell the difference between kind and harsh, and know the difference between justice and injustice—better than Aristotle does, apparently. They are even able to rise above retaliation, as Peter expects their behavior will not be determined by reaction to the behavior of others, but instead be, like God's own behavior, consistently governed by love. So how are they to direct their behavior in this situation?

Peter advises slaves using the same verb he has just used for the responsibility of every person toward every other person and of believers toward the institutions of government, the word he will later use for wives' relationships with their pagan husbands. All should *upotassō*. When addressing slaves and wives, he does not use a direct imperative; the verb is a participle. This ties the advice to slaves/wives, as specific applications, back to the general advice to all believers:[33] they should *upotassō*, and should do it

---

in court, and struck on the cheek, but not those who did the forcing, suing, or striking. This is because Jesus expects his followers won't be doing such things.

33. There is no small debate about 1 Peter's unconventional use of participles, much of it brought together in Thurén, *The rhetorical strategy*. Scholars generally agree that, in the two cases addressed here, the participle has the force of an exhortation, though there is still some debate about whether this

toward all things. Slaves are encouraged to do this "with all deference"; scholars of the language generally argue this refers to deference toward God, not toward the master,[34] as in the parallel usage regarding wives at 3:2–6.

Translating upotassō

Translators struggle to phrase an English rendering of *upotassō* that is faithful to the author's intent. It is striking that Peter does not in either of these cases employ Aristotle's verb, "obey." Peter is certainly familiar with that verb, since he uses it to invoke obedience (*hypakoē*) to God and to the gospel (1:2, 14, 22), even if this means rejecting the surrounding culture's norms.

Peter's verb for the behavior of everyone toward each other and the state, and of slaves toward their masters, and wives toward their husbands, suggests[35] finding and *occupying responsibly* one's place in society. It does not suggest resignation to the current ordering of that

form invokes a particular style of Tannaitic Hebrew common to the authors who were developing what would become the Mishnah between 10 and 220 CE. In that usage, participles in the place of imperatives convey "general ethical rules, denoting a custom." (Ibid., 10) "It never occurs when 'a specific person' is exhorted 'on a specific situation', nor in the case of an absolute law . . . it is used only in codes or in allusions to codes." (Ibid., 10) Daube (*Participle and Imperative*, 467–88) also suggests that 1 Peter only uses this construction when quoting from an earlier Jewish or Christian catechism. A quick review on the use of participles: We sometimes use a similar construction in English: "You have been such a kind friend during my illness! Picking me up at the hospital, carrying my things out to the car, even feeding my cat and watering my houseplants!" Using a main verb, followed by a string of explanatory but independent participles, is believed to be one first-century way of, in effect, writing bullet points. Scholars disagree concerning the weight of a participle used in this way, some arguing that "the imperativial participle is a softer command than the true imperative, more of an appeal than a directive." (Forbes, *1 Peter*, 6–7.) This would be consistent, generally, with Peter's verb choice at 2:11, the head of the household-code material: *parakaleō*, "I appeal to you," a verb used elsewhere in ancient writings to suggest one with authority who makes a winsome appeal rather than issuing an ultimatum.

34. For example, Ibid., 86.

35. Green, *1 Peter,* 73.

place. So a translation like "submit to" would be rather misleading; the New Testament, including this letter, elsewhere urges resistance and disobedience toward government and other institutions in some cases, and "submitting" would seem to be inconsistent with such disobeying and resisting. And in any case the first use of the word (2:13) would have each person doing this *toward every other person and thing*; it is logically impossible for each thing to obey every other thing as its ruler. Perhaps "be subordinate to" gets the sense of the Greek word. Or, to define by contrast, *upotassō* is the opposite of "withdrawing from," so perhaps "engage with" would be a fit translation. This does seem to be consistent with the general point of these sections of the letter: Followers of Jesus must engage with, not escape from, their social context.

Either "be obedient to" or "rebel against" would have been simpler instructions than "engage with." Obedience and rebellion appear to have been the most common reactions of first-century slaves to their predicament. Rebellion/resistance took many forms: assault of masters, refusing to defend masters when threatened, destruction of property, wasting time and defrauding masters, insolence, accepting bribery, suicide.[36] In fact, Roman law assumed these forms of rebellion, by assuming that being in the role of a slave inevitably led to loss of moral character.[37] Neither obedience nor disobedience require careful thought, but "engaging with" and "being subject to" do; they are complicated, as every citizen of a democracy knows. They require discernment, evaluation, being strategic, taking responsibility. Peter clarifies and qualifies "engaging with" in three ways: "because of the Lord" (2:13), "as persons having freedom," and "as God's slaves" (2:16).

Said differently, Peter has already indicated slavery is inconsistent with the new life of the church, that there is no inherent justice in the master-slave relationship (and in fact an inherent injustice), that the deliberative capacity of slaves may actually be superior to their unjust masters, that masters do not deserve

36. Bradley, *Slavery and Society at Rome*, 108–22; Krentz, "Order in the 'House' of God," 283.

37. Ibid.

unthinking obedience, that there are common virtues and standards for justice across social classes, that a slave's duty to a master is qualified by reverence for God (2:17, 19). Yet a person in the position of a slave has very few options. When mistreated, the two possibilities would seem to be resignation or rebellion (followed, frequently, by certain death). Peter tries to chart a different option—responsible engagement—and to associate it with meaning beyond the injustice inherent in the relationship.

Suffering and upotassō

²⁰If you endure when you are beaten for doing wrong, where is the credit in that? But if you endure when you do right and suffer for it, you have God's approval. ²¹For to this you have been called, because Christ also suffered for you, leaving you an example, so that you should follow in his steps.

> ²²'He committed no sin,
> and no deceit was found in his
> mouth.'

²³When he was abused, he did not return abuse; when he suffered, he did not threaten; but he entrusted himself to the one who judges justly. ²⁴He himself bore our sins in his body on the cross, so that, free from sins, we might live for righteousness; by his wounds you have been healed. ²⁵For you were going astray like sheep, but now you have returned to the shepherd and guardian of your souls.

It seems very likely that, when Peter speaks of doing right and suffering for it, he is referring to the mistreatment a slave might experience when he or she does not follow the *paterfamilias's* pagan cult. Slaves already had some legal standing to challenge other forms of mistreatment by masters; after saying that government exists to reward good behavior and punish bad behavior, and that mistreatment of slaves is in fact unjust bad behavior, it seems unlikely Peter would go on to say slaves have a general duty to not prosecute bad behavior when allowed to by law. But the expectation that slaves would follow the *paterfamilias's* pagan household cult was indeed a matter of law, and no Roman official would have viewed as improper the abuse of a Christian slave for following her or his own faith. Said differently, I don't believe Peter is laying down a general principle here that slaves must passively accept all mistreatment from their masters. Everywhere in this letter Peter speaks of "suffering" only when he means mistreatment that results from faithfulness to one's Christian profession; he does not enjoin generic suffering, as if it were somehow redemptive in itself, and he maintains that unjust suffering—even when it is a consequence of one's faith—is indeed an injustice, not something to be condoned or encouraged. Put more positively, every believer needs to remain faithful to their profession of faith and its implications, even if this is costly.

So Peter's point is not that "suffering is good for you," or that people should view suffering as morally neutral. He has already repeatedly used the word "injustice" for the experience he is describing. But when unavoidable suffering comes, suffering for which there is not presently any remedy, Peter invokes Isaiah 53 to remind the believing slave that all believers have a suffering master. In Christ, God has identified with the slave's suffering and shame; the word Peter uses for "beaten" is even the same word used in Mark's gospel for the beatings of Jesus. As a result of Jesus' identification, the slave has a new identity and dignity, and Jesus serves as an example of suffering for the truth, rather that capitulating or responding in kind. Either of those responses represents a deeper enslavement to the actions of the master; responding with integrity is, by contrast, freedom. Peter's advice repeats that of Jesus (e.g., Luke 6:32–35). Peter presents this as a principle in the economy of God's people.

Suffering and manumission

If Peter is threading the needle between slave rebellion and obedi-ence, by encouraging the engagement of *upotassō*, we might ask why he did not advocate a fourth option: manumission into free-dom. If Peter is convinced slavery is inconsistent with the Gospel, why does he not direct that the funds available for the support of widows also be used to free enslaved believers? Doesn't Paul seem to hint in this direction in his correspondence with Philemon?

The answer to this question probably also explains why the other, abbreviated household codes (in Colossians and Ephesians) say what they say and omit what they omit, relative to Peter's code. The horrible fact is manumission did not necessarily entail a bet-ter life than overt slavery.[38] Manumitted slaves were not free to go and do as they wished. They were expected to remain a part of the empire's patronage system. A "freed" slave must check in on her or his former master each morning to receive a list of assigned chores, and must make some public proclamation of the benefi-cence of the former master. Perhaps the patron would give a gift for this service, perhaps not; there was certainly no obligation on the part of the former master. The coercion over the former slave might well be more manipulative than before, when the master was at least obliged to feed, clothe, and house the slave. Though we have evidence that some manumitted slaves did become well off, either because they entered slavery as political captives with valuable skills, or because they acquired such skills as slaves and were able to leverage them after manumission, we also know very few former slaves were able to do so, and virtually none were ever accepted by society as equals. Most, especially unattached women, were pushed into a miserable urban underclass. Augus-tus so feared the magnitude of this potential political threat that he severely restricted the ability of households to manumit slaves upon the death of the *paterfamilias*. I believe it is for these reasons Peter rejects slavery and its ideological basis without calling for widespread manumission.

---

38. See, e.g., Koester, *Introduction to the New Testament*, 61–62.

Aristotle on masters

[Absent master section]

III.6: The rule of a master, although the slave by nature and the master by nature have in reality the same interests, is nevertheless exercised primarily with a view to the interest of the master, but accidentally considers the slave, since, if the slave perish, the rule of the master perishes with him . . . I.7: The rule of a household is a monarchy, for every house is under one head: whereas constitutional rule is a government of freemen and equals.

I have included here Aristotle's discussion of the slave-master's right to own others. There is obviously no parallel passage in 1 Peter. You can see Aristotle puts the master's interests first. A slave's survival is only interesting because without this the *paterfamilias* cannot be a slave-owner/*paterfamilias*. Aristotle also repeats his argument that the *polis* is a democracy among equals (*patres familia*), whereas an *oikos* must be a monarchy/tyranny.

To wives

I have added a few parenthetical comments in the following quotations, to provide context.

[1]Wives, in the same way, accept the authority of your (own) husbands, so that, even if some of them do not obey the word, they may be won over without a word by their wives' conduct, [2]when they see the purity and reverence of your lives. [3]Do not adorn yourselves outwardly by braiding your hair, and by wearing gold ornaments or fine clothing; [4]rather, let your adornment be the inner self with the lasting beauty of a gentle and quiet spirit, which is very precious in God's sight. [5]It was in this way long ago that the holy women who hoped in God used to adorn themselves by accepting the authority of (again, *upotassō*) their husbands. [6]Thus Sarah obeyed Abraham and called him lord. You have become her daughters as long as you do what is good and never let fears alarm you.

I.5: Again, the male is by nature superior, and the female inferior; and the one rules, and the other is ruled; ... I.12: A husband and father, we saw, rules over wife and children, both free, but the rule differs, the rule over his children being a royal, over his wife a constitutional rule ... The male is by nature fitter for command than the female, just as the elder and full-grown is superior to the younger and more immature ... There the inequality is permanent. The rule of a father over his children is royal, for he rules by virtue both of love and of the respect due to age, exercising a kind of royal power ... I.13: Clearly, then, moral virtue belongs to all of them; but the temperance of a man and of a woman, or the courage and justice of a man and of a woman, are not, as Socrates maintained, the same; the courage of a man is shown in commanding, of a woman in obeying. And this holds of all other virtues, as will be more clearly seen if we look at them in detail, for those who say generally that virtue consists in a good disposition of the soul, or in doing rightly, or the like, only deceive themselves.

I.13: Although the parts of the soul are present in all of them (male, female, child, slave), they are present in different degrees ... So it must necessarily be supposed to be with the moral virtues also; all should partake of them, but only in such manner and degree as is required by each for the fulfillment of his duty.

Peter introduces his paragraphs to wives (and later to husbands) with an identical thought: "In the same way . . . " His argument is based on the notion that all of these demographic groups share the same essential nature and a unity in Christ, as portrayed in the atonement. Thus there is commonality in the ways they will behave toward outsiders.

The verb used to counsel the wives of unbelieving *patres familias* is, as we've seen, not "obey" as with Aristotle, but the complex "engage/be subject to," and Peter pointedly limits it to one's own husband (*idiois andrasin*), not men in general. This is paired to a nice use of irony: In this sentence, it is the *husbands* who are faulted for not obeying. Wives are to meet their husbands' attitudes not with compliance, but with purity and reverence of life (which Aristotle ridicules here). This purity and reverence to God will sometimes involve disobedience of the husband, because of the pagan husband's priestly responsibilities. The potential disobedience required by purity and reverence is then filled out by a case or two. Peter counsels against the adornments of braided hair, gold ornaments, and fine clothing, replacing them with the inner adornment of a gentle and quiet spirit, and the outer practice of doing what is good.

Sarah is invoked as a model, eventually using the verb "obey," in another instance of wry wit. Peter has referenced the Hebrew Scriptures so frequently and subtly that he must be confident his readers knew them well. Likely they would recall the only place in which Sarah refers to Abraham as "lord" is in the context of bemusement, not docile obedience: a visitor tells the elderly couple they will have a child, and Sarah laughs: "After I have grown old, and my lord is old, shall I have pleasure?" (Gen 18:12) In fact, the Septuagint Genesis uses the word "obey" of Abraham toward Sarah (16:2), but never of Sarah toward Abraham. Abraham had been repeatedly disobedient (chapters 12 and 20) to God in ways that belittled and endangered Sarah while they both lived as aliens and sojourners. At Genesis 21:12, God finally tells Abraham to obey whatever Sarah instructs him to do.

We can feel some of the struggle faced by the women in Peter's churches when we read the quotation from Aristotle. Aristotle's is a world of male rule and unquestioning female obedience, justified by superior male temperance and courage; the surrounding culture generally viewed women as dominated by emotions, and therefore given to immorality, intemperance, greediness, and contentiousness.[39] In fact, Aristotle says in so many words that he is hostile to the notion of virtue being a gentle and quiet disposition of the soul, or even of virtue consisting of doing what is right![40] Perhaps it is no wonder the world of the *paterfamilias* came to be associated with such debauchery. Yet Peter encourages persistence, even in the face of intimidation:[41] "Never let fears alarm you" is phrased quite emphatically, with the equivalent of a double-negation. Do what is right, even if this is different from the things your husband commands.

It may not be apparent to modern readers that Peter's counsel about dress and jewelry may amount to *disobedience* of the *paterfamilias* and empowerment of the woman. But try reading it the other way: "Women, don't wear jewelry or nice clothing, because you know your pagan husbands hate that sort of thing and have commanded you not to do it." That doesn't make any sense. In fact we know the surrounding culture placed tremendous emphasis on displays of jewelry and finery, as an outward expression of the wealth of the *oikos* and the prominence of the *paterfamilias*.

---

39. If not clear enough from Aristotle, summarized well by Achtemeier, *1 Peter*, 206.

40. We do have comments from some other schools of Hellenistic thought that do affirm the same qualities, virtues, and behaviors Peter here affirms, and also hold out (in principle) duties for wives that affirm their deliberative and administrative capacities. This does not impinge upon the argument I am making here; in fact, it strengthens the argument that Peter is making a case against the Aristotilian household-code tradition. And Peter's dissent exceeds even the more generous alternative traditions. For example, the *Pythagorean Letter of Melissa to Clearete* argues against wifely adornment on the grounds that it makes the wife look like a prostitute, then goes on to counsel: "The husband's will ought to be engraved as law on a decent wife's mind, and she must live by it." (Horsley, *New Documents Illustrating Early Christianity*, 6)

41. Forbes, *1 Peter*, 103.

Now put yourself in the shoes of a female convert in one of Peter's churches, married to a pagan *paterfamilias*. Your daily reality is some mixture of these elements: you were married as a property arrangement between two families. In Roman culture (unlike our review of Jewish Palestinian culture) you were married just after puberty to a man twice your age, who has the freedom to walk away when he wants; your only leverage is the dowry your *paterfamilias* paid to him, which would go back to your *paterfamilias*, not you. Upon marriage you renounced your father's religion and agreed to worship only at your new husband's hearth—you would not make friends of your own, but enjoy your husband's friends, the first of which were his gods.[42] At the moment, he has title to all of your possessions. He occasionally has a child by you, but spends much of his intimate time with young women or younger boys. You have taken up a new Christian religion that transfers the Emperor's titles to a convicted insurrectionist, and this religion requires that you not participate in your husband's cult religion, which he is legally responsible to impose on you. And now he (or his *paterfamilias*) wants you to dress in a way that flaunts the wealth of his estate. This includes, in Nero's day and the decades that followed, the use of grandiose curly wigs fashioned from the hair of slaves, sometimes built upon grand internal wooden frames. Peter's advice: when your man wants to turn you into that kind of object, you should disobey, and you'll have the authority and fellowship of the church behind your refusal. Peter's injunction is against conforming to aristocratic culture when it trivializes people, people created in God's image.

42. Green, *1 Peter*, 92–93; Plutarch, *Coniug. praec.* 19.140D. Some also reference Plutarch's comments that the wife's adornment should be not cosmetics or finery but "those things that put forward gravity that commands respect, being in the correct social posture" (*Coniug. Praec.* 19.141E) to suggest that Peter is only repeating and slightly modifying Plutarch in 3:3–4. (See, e.g., Krentz, "Order in the 'House' of God," 284.) But, in light of Aristotle, "gravity and commands respect. . . in the correct social posture" would hardly be the things Peter enjoins. Furthermore, Plutarch was born around 46 CE, and would not have even begun his education in philosophy at the time we are dating the writing of 1 Peter; it is more likely, though unlikely, that Plutarch is quoting Peter than Peter is amending Plutarch.

Note that this all comes immediately after the call to "engage/ be subordinate to" the authority of the husband. Thus the husband's authority is clearly not absolute; it does not even extend to issues of clothing and hair style. Again, Peter presumes deliberative capacity among women that is at least equal to that of their husbands.

We must think through one last nuance in this paragraph about wives and husbands. The groups directly addressed by Aristotle and Peter are "slaves," "wives," and "husbands." For Aristotle's household code, the "wife" and "husband" would be in the singular, addressing the *paterfamilias* and his spouse. The other (non-family) wives and husbands on the estate would generally fall under the category of "slaves." So when Peter uses the genre of a household code to address Christian congregations, whom should we think of when we hear people addressed as "wives?"

Our natural modern tendency is to hear this as counsel addressed to all married women, but it is likely that Peter's congregations consisted primarily of rural tenant farmers who worked the land of large household-estates,[43] thus most of the recipients were likely not slaves, but also not Aristotle's "husband" (*paterfamilias*) or his "wife." They were instead the Empire's majority vanquished working class, not slaves but not citizens, not able to vote or own land or hold most political or priestly offices, with limited legal protections (especially concerning marriage and transfers of property), subject to military draft and fully taxed.[44]

If we put this all differently, in the genre Peter is using here, it is possible the majority of the congregation would not recognize themselves as being directly addressed.[45] They are not, in this genre's usage, slaves or wives (of the *paterfamilias*) or husbands (that is, a *paterfamilias*). So why would Peter write a letter that does not directly address most of the recipients? Because, I believe, his main intent is to critique the culture surrounding the congregation, by critiquing the way culture thinks about things like persons,

---

43. See, e.g., Elliott, *A Home for the Homeless,* 63.

44. Ibid., 68, 71.

45. Perhaps this explains why the next section begins with "Finally, all of you, ..."

households, economies, social standing, slavery, marriage, wealth, and patronage. Peter's household code is not only instruction for personal behavior within individual, specific household estates; it is a pattern for countercultural behavior across the entire church. This church is the "household of God" in the same sense that it is the "house of Jacob" with which God has made covenant and lived (e.g., Exod 19:3, referenced at 1 Peter 2:9), liberating it from the "house of bondage" (Exod 13, 20).

If these congregations had already come across Paul's 1 Corinthians, they would have seen there a complementary discussion—which does not appear to be limited to the case of *paterfamilias* and spouse—of marriages between a believing wife and a pagan husband. Paul similarly begins by encouraging virtuous behavior. Then he says if the husband is willing to accept all the profound challenges to his behavior that come with his wife's conversion, the two should remain married; if not, the wife should not feel bound by the marriage. That is certainly not a recipe for the stereotypically obedient, submissive wife. Paul seems to go out of his way to repeat exactly the same advice for wives as for husbands.[46]

To free men

Peter now, finally, turns his attention to the free men in the congregation.

> [7]Husbands, in the same way, show
> consideration for your wives in
> your life together, paying honor to
> the woman as the weaker sex, since
> they too are also heirs of the gra-
> cious gift of life—so that nothing
> may hinder your prayers.

46. "If any believer has a wife who is an unbeliever, and she consents to live with him, he should not divorce her. And if any woman has a husband who is an unbeliever, and he consents to live with her, she should not divorce him . . . If the unbelieving partner separates, let it be so; in such a case the brother or sister is not bound." (1 Cor 7:12–15)

I have not included a parallel passage from Aristotle for this short paragraph, because there isn't one. We have already seen his advice for men, and it certainly does not begin with "In the same way (as slaves and women) . . . "

The phrase "in the same way" is slightly different than was the case with wives and slaves (here involving an article), which may suggest a more direct mirroring of the responsibilities between husband and wife[47], though Peter does not use the verb *upotassō* in this sentence.

There may be a gentle put-down of Aristotle in Peter's opening phrase. Often translated "live with your wives with consideration/understanding," it could be rendered more literally as "live with ("your wife" is implied) according to knowledge."[48] For all of Aristotle's protestations that he is only doing what is rational, his arguments are really not that smart; they are built on stereotypes and the projection of weaknesses onto others.

Peter reminds us that husband and wife are both inheritors in this new *oikos,* and specifically mentions "a life together" as part of the marriage covenant. Didymus had dropped this notion from Aristotle, arguing that marriage was simply a necessity for procreation. Aristotle, while allowing that a life together was a positive part of marriage, argues marriage exists because of the animal-like desire for sex, basing his argument on extrapolations from animal and plant behavior. Peter does not place procreation or desire as the basis for marriage. Instead, consideration and honor are central.

Saying honor should be shown to the physically weaker sex is a nice reversal of Plato/Aristotle's conception of *timocracy,* which directs honor (*timos*) toward the physically strong, especially those who have killed others in warfare. The "weakness" of women, given the presumption of equal deliberative capacity in the prior paragraphs, surely indicates relative physical weakness[49] and the

47. Forbes, *1 Peter,* 103.

48. Ibid., 104, argues this is the better translation.

49. Peter's contemporary, Musonius Rufus, uses the same phrase and fully expounds that by it he means a generalization about average physical strength,

concomitant threat of physical abuse; a better translation would be "as the weaker body."[50]

Peter really doesn't have much to say to men *as men*. He has already said it. A simple "see the above" is about all that is required.

Three poems for the entire church

As it began, Peter's code ends with a joint address to all, as possessing a common nature.

[8]Finally, all of you,

have unity of spirit,
　　sympathy,
　　　　love for one another,
　　a tender heart,
and a humble mind.

[9]Do not repay evil for evil or abuse for abuse;
　　but, on the contrary, repay with a blessing.
It is for this that you were called—
　　that you might inherit a blessing.

[10]For "those who desire life
and desire to see good days,

　　let them keep their tongues from evil
　　and their lips from speaking deceit;

　　　　[11]let them turn away from evil and do good;
　　　　let them seek peace and pursue it.

　　[12]For the eyes of the Lord are on the righteous,
　　and his ears are open to their prayer.

But the face of the Lord is against those who do evil."

---

a generalization not meant to characterize every individual. (Rufus, "Should Daughters Receive the Same Educations as Sons?" in Lutz, "Musonius Rufus," 51–59.

　　50. Forbes, *1 Peter,* 103–4.

This section closes the code with three things: a chiastic exhortation that summarizes life within the fellowship; a psalmlike poem that summarizes behavior toward the surrounding culture; and a chiastic quotation from Psalm 34 to close the entire household code section.

Peter's vocative transition—"Finally, all of you"—emphasizes he is no longer addressing components of the fellowship in their dealings with pagans, but now the common humanity within the fellowship. The Greek words attached to "all of you" are usually translated "Finally, . . . " even though we are nowhere near the end of the letter. We could render the phrase more literally (and more in line with his similar usage at 4:7) as "So the *telos* (completion, goal, consummation), all of you, is same-thinkingness, cosuffering, . . . " Peter uses five words in a chiasm to characterize the *telos* of life together as God's new humanity in the resurrected Christ:

Being like-minded (*homophrones*),

    Being sympathetic, with like feelings in suffering (*sympatheis*[51])

        Loving each other as siblings (*philadelphoi*[52]),

    Being tender-hearted, with compassion for each other (*eusplagchnoi*),

Being humble-minded (*tapeinophrones*).

You can see the classical Greek three-theme analysis of the soul being toyed with again: the first and last words allude to thinking, the second and fourth to feeling/desire. At the focal point of the chiasm, and in place of Plato/Aristotle's third element of the soul (appetite), Paul places *love*—not a craving that consumes and exploits, but real love that honors and seeks the good of others. Love is ultimately what structures this new humanity in Christ. (This is reiterated at 4:8.)

---

51. So far as we know, Peter is coining a phrase here; this word does not occur elsewhere in the New Testament, and there are no pre-Christian uses either. (Elliott, *A Home for the Homeless*, 136)

52. This word usage, suggestive of household relationships, is also unique to Peter in the New Testament.

The next sentences, Peter's summary of life among hostile pagans, are gracious: where possible, do not repay evil or abuse in kind. Repay with blessing.

The final quotation from Psalm 34 forms another chiasm. The first idea—life and good days for the righteous—is mirrored in the last line—judgement of those who are not righteous. The second idea (tongues that are righteous and straightforward) finds its fulfillment in the fourth idea, God's ears being open to those tongues' prayers. All four verses point toward the primary idea, in the middle: turn from evil, do good, seek peace.

You'll have noticed Peter has not yet raised any discussion of the parent-child, older-younger theme in Aristotle's household code. I believe this is because he has used the household-code genre to discuss relationships of believers toward those *outside* of the covenant community. The New Testament views the children of believers as a part of the covenant people, even for the case in which only one parent is a believer. (Paul's 1 Corinthians 7, for example, makes this especially clear.) Peter will indeed discuss relationships between older and younger within the fellowship, but he separates that discussion from the formal household code by about thirty verses of commentary.

Peter's interlude

That interval is a remarkable remix of topics. Peter takes phrases from his household code, splices them into phrases from his introductory section, weaves in references to second-temple Jewish literature, and touches on an assortment of other principles, injunctions, and doctrines. This is not the place for a full exposition of these verses, but we should note one theme: the words of instruction that were given to slaves are now universalized to all the believers' dealings with others (3:13–14, 3:17–18, 4:1–2, 4:12–16, 4:19),[53] as are the instructions to wives (3:14–16). It was not simply

53. "Finally, all of you, . . . Who will harm you if you are eager to do what is good? But even if you do suffer for doing what is right, you are blessed . . . Keep your conscience clear, so that, when you are maligned, those who abuse you for

to the slave *as a slave* or the wife *as a wife* that those words about returning good for evil were given, though the slave's and wife's contexts are unique; these are the same principles by which anyone in the fellowship should live. To emphasize this universality, Peter switches (4:10) from the master-slave/husband-wife categories of Aristotle's code to two other household-office references, applied to all believers: "Like good stewards (*oikonomoi,* managers of the household) of the manifold grace of God, serve (*diakonountes,* enacting the routine, so-called "menial" chores of household servants) one another with whatever gift each of you has received."

Chapter 5 begins with Peter's discussion for elders and youth, which I place in parallel with some of Aristotle's comments on the same topics (with one parenthetical note added by me for context).

---

your good conduct in Christ may be put to shame. For it is better to suffer for doing good, if suffering should be God's will, than to suffer for doing evil. For Christ also suffered for sins once for all, the righteous for the unrighteous, in order to bring you to God . . . Since therefore Christ suffered in the flesh, arm yourselves also with the same intention (for whoever has suffered in the flesh has finished with sin), so as to live for the rest of your earthly life no longer by human desires but by the will of God . . . Beloved, do not be surprised at the fiery ordeal that is taking place among you to test you, as though something strange were happening to you. But rejoice in so far as you are sharing Christ's sufferings, so that you may also be glad and shout for joy when his glory is revealed. If you are reviled for the name of Christ, you are blessed, because the spirit of glory, which is the Spirit of God, is resting on you. But let none of you suffer as a murderer, a thief, a criminal, or even as a mischief-maker. Yet if any of you suffers as a Christian, do not consider it a disgrace, but glorify God because you bear this name . . . Therefore, let those suffering in accordance with God's will entrust themselves to a faithful Creator, while continuing to do good."

Elders and youth

Now as an elder myself and a witness of the sufferings of Christ, as well as one who shares in the glory to be revealed, I exhort the elders among you ²to tend the flock of God that is in your charge, exercising the oversight, not under compulsion but willingly, as God would have you do it—not for sordid gain but eagerly. ³Do not lord it over those in your charge, but be examples to the flock. ⁴And when the chief shepherd appears, you will win the crown of glory that never fades away. ⁵In the same way, you who are younger must accept the authority of the elders.

And all of you must clothe yourselves with humility in your dealings with one another, for "God opposes the proud,

but gives grace to the humble."

⁶Humble yourselves therefore under the mighty hand of God, so that he may exalt you in due time.

I.12: A husband and father, we saw, rules over wife and children, both free, but the rule differs, the rule over his children being a royal ... The male is by nature fitter for command than the female, just as the elder and full-grown is superior to the younger and more immature ... There the inequality is permanent. The rule of a father over his children is royal, for he rules by virtue both of love and of the respect due to age, exercising a kind of royal power ...

I.13: Although the parts of the soul are present in all of them (male, female, child, slave), they are present in different degrees ... So it must necessarily be supposed to be with the moral virtues also; all should partake of them, but only in such manner and degree as is required by each for the fulfillment of his duty.

For Aristotle, elders rule as royal dictators over the younger. (Did Aristotle really need to say it this many times?!) The older man is by nature more virtuous, more rational, and more deserving of obedience, and therefore obliged to command.

Peter, like Jesus, rejects this scheme. (Though Peter might have been expected to adopt it, since he is the undisputed leader of the disciples, it would be very odd if he actually did in this letter, since the Gospel of Mark so clearly rejects it in chapter 10, and that gospel is a collaboration between the same authors, Peter and Mark.) Elders have a responsibility because of what they have witnessed. That responsibility involves tending a flock (recalling

Jesus' word that a good shepherd lays down his life for the sheep), willingly exercising oversight, not seeking financial or social gain, not lording it over others. In sum, an elder is to be an example, which is to say the elder lives just as the younger should live, not trying to live a life apart and somehow superior. This is the nature of legitimate authority.

Said differently, Peter explicitly rejects an inference that some elders might have drawn: because Jesus rules all creation authoritatively (3:22), shouldn't that hierarchy find an echo in earthly relationships? Should not elders rule the younger just as Christ rules the church? And, by extension, should not masters rule slaves and husbands rule wives, expecting the same obedience that Christ expects of the church? No. Elders are shepherds, not kings. Husbands show consideration and honor "in the same way" wives and slaves do. Paul rejects male-kingship in a similar way: husbands take as their model not the ascended, reigning Christ, but the self-emptying, suffering Jesus. (Eph 5:25)

Those who are younger are addressed directly, and receive a very brief guideline: they should "in the same way *upotassō*." There is that phrase again! This is neither obedience nor rebellion, but responsibly finding one's place.

Then comes a longer, last section, addressed to both groups, imploring humility. Having rejected Aristotle's social arrangement between young and old, Peter now rejects its basis: the presumption of automatic improvement in virtue as one ages. The greatest of sins is pride, the greatest of virtues, humility. This is precisely what Aristotle missed. The word used for the humility in which all must be clothed (*enkombōsasthe*) appears to be a variant of the word for a slave's apron.

Peter's goodbye

Peter closes the body of the letter with brief reminders: don't worry, but do be self-controlled. Then, as is typical of New Testament letters, comes a doxology: "To God be the power for ever and ever. Amen."

A short epilogue, apparently written in Peter's own hand, identifies Sylvanus and Mark as collaborators, refers to his location as "Babylon" (a fitting name for Rome in a letter so critical of its ideology), and echoes the letter's opening line by wishing the readers peace.

I have argued that, by letter's end, Peter has overturned the dominant culture's view of household relationships, which amounted to overturning the culture's dominant economic ideology. This interpretation of Peter's letter is consistent with what we know of the succeeding decades of church practice. The Christian church gradually abandoned the structure of meeting in homes, which had initially been its principal *modus operandi.* There were two prominent reasons:[54] First, despite Peter's instruction, household heads continued to exert too much influence, especially over decisions about who would receive hospitality from the church. (This tension is already apparent in, for example, 2 John 10–11, 3 John 9–10, Jas 2:1–13, 1 Cor 11:17–34.) Second, the culture's household roles were too rigidly defined to be consistent with the church's gospel, particularly for wives, unmarried women, and slaves.

54. For example, see Craddock, *First and Second Peter and Jude,* 49.

6

Epilogue

WE BEGAN BY LOOKING at the very long shadow cast by Aristotle's economic theory of the household, a shadow that darkens even modern American culture. The length of that shadow was extended by the widespread belief that the New Testament's household codes amount to an endorsement of Aristotle's ideas. As we saw, even the majority of contemporary New Testament scholarship proceeds under this assumption.

I have argued this is a mistaken reading of the New Testament codes. One needn't reject the New Testament witness as a slavery-condoning, misogynistic embarrassment, nor argue the New Testament authors strategically endorsed structures they knew to be immoral and inconsistent with their gospel. And one needn't endorse Aristotle's attitudes toward women, marginalized populations, and child-rearing out of a sense that these attitudes are endorsed in the New Testament.

If this is true, how did the church get from Point A to Point B—from a witty rejection of Aristotle to a conviction that the Scriptures endorse him? That discussion is worthy of its own book, but let us sketch the story here.

We know the second century was very formative for the doctrines, ethics, and liturgy that became prominent in the Christian church,[1] and it appears fundamental changes were at work already in that century, suggesting a divergence from Peter's Epistle.

There are indications that, initially in the second century, there was continuity between the interpretation I've suggested for 1 Peter and the practices of the church in general. For example, despite an imperial ban until the fourth century on the Christian movement's ownership of property, the church gradually abandoned the structure of meeting in homes. This was a radical change for a movement that has been called a "social world in the making," one that had relied heavily upon the structure of the household for its propagation. As we've seen, the abandonment of the household structure appears to have been motivated by[2] *patres familias* exerting too much influence, and the rigidly-defined household code roles of the surrounding *oikos* culture; these roles came to be viewed as inhibiting Christian liberty, particularly for wives, unmarried women, and slaves.

The letter of Polycarp to the Philippians (composed around 110–140 CE) also maintained Peter's language of mutual *upotassomenai*: "All of you, submit yourselves to one another, having your manner above reproach."[3] And Justin Martyr (100–165 CE), in his disputation with Trypho (around 155–165), famously defended a high view of the place of women in the people of God.[4]

But an alternative narrative was gradually developing. Already Clement, Bishop of Rome (88–99 CE) was influenced by the Roman Empire's absorption of the Second Sophistic movement

1. For example, see Bingham and Jefford, *Intertextuality in the Second Century*, 1.

2. Craddock, *First and Second Peter and Jude*, 49.

3. Polycarp, "Epistle to the Philippians," 10:2.

4. Brief fragments of the New Testament codes also seem to appear at *Didache* (probably first half of second century CE) 4:10–11 (concerning slavery); *1 Clement* (perhaps a disciple of Peter) 1:3 (concerning mutual submission, women, and wives) and 21:6–9 (regarding women and children); *Epistle of Barnabas* (probably early second century CE) 19:7 (on slavery); and Polycarp's *Philippians* (first half of second century CE) 4:2 (regarding wives). Parallels to some Jewish and Stoic codes are discussed in Kelly, *The Epistles of Peter and of Jude*, 107–8.

that repopularized Aristotle. His Letter to the Corinthians elevates leaders and elders relative to wives and the young, and (shockingly, given Emperor Domitian's persecutions reflected in Revelation) speaks of Roman imperial rule as part of the natural concord of God's creation, to be obeyed as God himself, not merely honored because believers should honor fellow humans. By the time of Tertullian (155–240 CE), who nominally endorsed a hard rejection of Greek thought, the Aristotelian view of women had resurfaced and was being advocated. Tertullian memorably portrayed women as a public menace, perpetually subject to God's curse on Eve. By the fourth century, Jerome (b. 347) could speak of women as "the root of all evil," even though he was dependent upon the work of women for "his" famous and history-changing translation work.

So it appears by the end of the second century the Second Sophistic movement, which we referenced in Chapter 3, was beginning to exert a long-term influence in the theology of the Christian church. This set of changes is probably related to changing demographics within the Christian movement:

> The spectrum of beliefs . . . was not broad at the outset . . . This began to change when the Jewish Christian presence in the movement began to dwindle and become a small minority, and there arose non-Jewish ideas, voices, and prejudices against things Jewish in the second century and later.[5]

This dynamic appears to have influenced not only attitudes about women but also, in the long run, dispositions toward slavery. Though there were periodic pleas that slavery be abolished[6] or that slavery was unnatural and should be limited,[7] and though in some places churches used church funds to liberate slaves, the practice of slavery lived on. The numbers of enslaved persons dwindled, partly because of Christian opposition, which became more effective after Constantine elevated Christianity to protected

---

5. Witherington, *Invitation to the New Testament,* 37.

6. For example, from Gregory of Nyssa, Acacius of Amida, and Saint Patrick.

7. For example, from Origen, Augustine, and John Chrysostom.

status early in the fourth century and granted bishops' courts the right to manumit slaves.[8] Ancient Roman slavery also declined because of changing economic forces. Beginning in the third century, aristocratic households increasingly became economically marginalized, and this made slavery more expensive than relying upon dependent sharecropping serfs.

As the modern era caused serfdom to recede and colony-based nation-building to emerge, the new financial and political motives for enslavement required a new, intellectually respectable justification. Thus began the modern reincarnation of Aristotle's ideology of slavery, served in the fifteenth century by several papal bulls and, in 1517, by a Bishop's request to commence the transatlantic trade in African slaves.

If later events and ideologies have eclipsed 1 Peter's intentions, there is no reason to remain in that imposed darkness. Peter spoke into an era in which personal identity was caught up in stereotypes about gender, ethnicity, age, and class. He points to a different way. When one's identity, one's primary source of self, is found as a sibling in a community framed by God's love, many things become possible: respecting others, seeking their good, deferring to their interests, laughing at the world's standards of privilege. And many things become impossible: lording it over others, thinking of privilege as a gain, redefining the standards of justice to one's own advantage. Peter had learned the hard way, in his early life as a disciple, that prideful overconfidence and reliance upon one's privileged status led to epic, crushing failure. He had been forced to face his own cowardice and cruelty, to receive a new and true identity not built upon his own sense of superiority or his willful commitment to a cause. He had pursued being his own savior, and it had not saved him. In fact, it had misled him, and left him inconsolable when it all fell apart. So in his major epistle he reminds his flock that theirs is a received identity, a communal identity, a gift grounded in God's demonstrated love for them.

---

8. However, even through the medieval period, Christian opposition to slavery was often limited to the plight of *Christian* slaves.

In the first century, this rubbed against Aristotle's impulse to find one's identity in some sense of superiority based on gender, age, and ethnicity—Aristotle's authoritarian trinity of husband, father, and master. In the twenty-first century, the Aristotelian impulse still has its advocates. Some of the church's most influential leadership counsel male superiority relative to women, strong parental authoritarianism toward children, and social constructions that reinforce racial/ethnic privilege. As we have seen, this impulse is denounced by Peter's great epistle.

Bibliography

Achtemeier, Paul J. *1 Peter: A Commentary on First Peter*. Hermeneia: A Critical and Historical Commentary on the Bible. Minneapolis: Fortress, 1996.

Arieti, James A. *Philosophy and the Ancient World: An Introduction*. Lanham, MD: Rowman and Littlefield, 2005.

Aristotle. *Politics*. Edited by H. W. Carless Davis. Translated by Benjamin Jowett. Oxford: Clarendon, 1920.

Balch, David L. *Let Wives be Submissive: The Domestic Code in 1 Peter*. Society of Biblical Literature Monograph Series 26. Chico, CA: Scholars, 1981.

Benedict XVI, Pope. "*Lectio Divnia* of the Holy Father Benedict." http://w2.vatican.va/content/benedict-xvi/en/speeches/2013/february/documents/hf_ben-xvi_spe_20130208_seminario-romano-mag.html.

Best, Ernest. *1 Peter*. New Century Bible. Sheffield: Sheffield Academic, 1971.

Bingham, D. Jeffrey, and Clayton N. Jefford, eds. *Intertextuality in the Second Century*. Leiden, the Netherlands: Brill Academic, 2016.

Bradley, Keith. *Slavery and Society at Rome*. Cambridge: Cambridge University Press, 1994.

Brent, Allen. "Ignatius of Antioch in Second Century Asia Minor." In *Intertextuality in the Second Century*, edited by Jeffrey D. Bingham and Clayton N. Jefford, 62–86. Leiden, the Netherlands: Brill Academic, 2016.

Brown, Raymond E. *An Introduction to the New Testament*. The Anchor Yale Bible Reference Library. New Haven, CT: Yale University Press. 1997.

Brownmiller, Susan. *Against Our Will: Men, Women and Rape*. New York: Simon and Schuster, 1975.

Cary, Otis, and Frank Cary. "How Old were Christ's Disciples?" *The Biblical World* 50 (1917) 3–12.

Clowney, Edmund. *The Message of 1 Peter*. The Bible Speaks Today. Leicester, UK: InterVarsity, 1988.

Cohen, Adam S. "Harvard's Eugenics Era." *Harvard Magazine* March–April 2016. http://harvardmagazine.com/2016/03/harvards-eugenics-era.

Corley, Kathleen E. "1 Peter." In *Searching the Scriptures*, vol. 2, *A Feminist Commentary*, edited by Elisabeth Schüssler Fiorenza, 349–60. New York: Crossroad, 1994.

Craddock, Fred B. *First and Second Peter and Jude*. Louisville: Westminster John Knox, 1995.

Cranfield, C. E. B. *The First Epistle of Peter*. London: SCM, 1950.

Crouch, James E. *The Origin and Intention of the Colossian Haustafel*. Göttingen, Germany: Vandenhoeck & Ruprecht, 1972.

Daube, D. "Appended Note: Participle and Imperative in I Peter." In *The First Epistle of St. Peter*, 2nd ed., edited by E. G. Selwyn, 467–88. London: Macmillan, 1947.

Donelson, Lewis R. *I & II Peter and Jude: A Commentary*. Louisville: Westminster John Knox, 2010.

Dormeyer, Detlev. *The New Testament Among the Writings of Antiquity*. Sheffield, UK: Sheffield Academic, 1998.

Dudrey, Russ. "'Submit Yourselves to One Another': A Social-Historical Look at the Household Code of Ephesians 5:15—6:9." *Restoration Quarterly* 41 (1999) 27–44.

Elliott, John H. *1 Peter: A New Translation with Introduction and Commentary*. Anchor Bible 37B. New York: Doubleday, 2000.

———. *A Home for the Homeless: A Sociological Exegesis of 1 Peter, its Situation and Strategy*. Philadelphia: Fortress, 1981.

Elliott, Robert C. "Satire." In *Encyclopedia Britannica*. https://www.britannica.com/art/satire.

Fiorenza, Elizabeth Schüssler. *1 Peter: Reading Against the Grain*. Phoenix Guides to the New Testament 18. Sheffield, UK: Sheffield Phoenix, 2015.

Foner, Eric. *Gateway to Freedom: The Hidden History of the Underground Railroad*. New York: W. W. Norton, 2015.

Forbes, Greg W. *1 Peter*. Exegetical Guide to the Greek New Testament. Nashville: B&H Academic, 2014.

Freyne, Sean. *Galilee from Alexander the Great to Hadrian 323 BCE to 135 CE: A Study of Second Temple Judaism*. Edinburgh: T&T Clark, 1998.

Glaeser, Edward I. "Urban Colossus: Why is New York America's Largest City?" *FRB New York Economic Policy Review* 11 (Dec 2005), 9–14.

Gombis, Timothy G. "A Radically Different New Humanity: The Function of the *Haustafel* in Ephesians." *Journal of the Evangelical Theological Society* 48 (2005) 317–30.

Goppelt, L. *Der erste Petrusbrief*. Kritisch-Exegetischer Kommentar über das Neue Testament 12/1. Göttingen, Germany: Vandenhoeck und Ruprecht, 1978.

Green, Joel B. *1 Peter*. Grand Rapids: Eerdmans, 2007.

Grudem, Wayne. *The First Epistle of Peter: An Introduction and Commentary*. Tyndale New Testament Commentaries. Leicester, UK: InterVarsity, 1988.

Harink, Douglas. *1 & 2 Peter*. Brazos Theological Commentary on the Bible. Grand Rapids: Brazos, 2009.

Harris, W. V. "Child-Exposure in the Roman Empire." *The Journal of Roman Studies* 84 (1994) 1–22.

Hills, Julian V., ed. *Common Life in the Early Church: Essays Honoring Graydon F. Snyder.* Harrisburg, PA: Trinity Press International, 1998.

Horsley, G. H. R. *New Documents Illustrating Early Christianity.* North Ryde, Australia: Macquarie University Press, 1982.

Judge, E. A. *The Social Pattern of Christian Groups in the First Century.* London: Tyndale, 1960.

Kamlah, E. "*Hypotassesthai* in den neutestamentlichen 'Haustafeln." In *Verborum Veritas, Festschrift für G. Stählin,* edited by O. Böcher and K. Haacker, 237–43. Wuppertal, Germany: Theologischer Verlag, 1970.

Keener, Craig. *Paul, Women, and Wives: Marriage and Women's Ministry in the Letters of Paul.* Peabody, MA: Hendrickson, 1992.

Kelly, J. N. D. *The Epistles of Peter and of Jude.* Black's New Testament Commentary 17. Grand Rapids: Baker Academic, 1969.

Koester, Helmut. *Introduction to the New Testament, Vol. 1: History, Culture, and Religion of the Hellenistic Age.* 2nd ed. New York: Walter de Gruyter, 1995.

Krentz, Edgar. "Order in the 'House' of God: The *Haustafel* in 1 Peter 2:11—3:12." In *Common Life in the Early Church: Essays Honoring Graydon F. Snyder,* edited by Julian V. Hills, 279–85. Harrisburg, PA: Trinity Press International, 1998.

Lincoln, Andrew Y. "The Household Code and Wisdom Mode of Colossians." *Journal for the Study of the New Testament* 74 (1999) 93–112.

Longenecker, Bruce W. *Remember the Poor: Paul, Poverty, and the Greco-Roman World.* Grand Rapids: Eerdmans, 2010.

Lutz, Cora E. "Musonius Rufus: 'The Roman Socrates." In *Yale Classical Studies* 10, edited by Alfred R. Bellinger, 3–150. New Haven: Yale University Press, 1947.

MacDonald, Margaret. *The Pauline Churches: A Socio-Historical Study of Institutionalization in the Pauline and Deutero-Pauline Writings.* Society for New Testament Studies Monograph Series 60. Cambridge: Cambridge University Press, 1988.

Nagel, D. Brendon. "Aristotle and Arius Didymus on Household and *POLIS.*" *Rheinisches Museum für Philologie* Neue Folge 145 (2002) 198–223.

Oxford Biblical Studies Online. "Household Codes." http://www.oxfordbiblicalstudies.com/article/opr/t94/e912.

Parsons, Michael. "Slavery and the New Testament: Equality and Submissiveness." *Vox Evangelica* 18 (1988) 90–96.

Philo. *The Cherubim.* Translated by Charles Duke Yonge. London: H. G. Bohn, 1854.

Plutarch. *Coniugalia Praecepta.* Translated by Frank Cole Babbitt. Loeb Classical Library 222. Cambridge, MA: Harvard University Press, 1928.

Polycarp. "Epistle to the Philippians." In *Early Christian Fathers,* translated and edited by Cyril C. Richardson, 131–40. New York: Touchstone, 1996.

Richards, E. Randolph. "Silvanus was not Peter's Secretary: The Theological Bias in Interpreting *dia Silouanou . . . egrapha* in 1 Peter 5:12." *Journal of the Evangelical Theological Society* 43 (2000) 417–32.

Scher, Bill. "Princeton, Don't Erase Woodrow Wilson's Name." November 23, 2015, RealClear Politics. https://www.realclearpolitics.com/articles/2015/11/23/princeton_dont_erase_woodrow_wilsons_name_128819.html.

Stagg, Frank. *New Testament Theology.* Nashville: Broadman, 1962.

Standhartinger, Angela. "The Origin and Intention of the Household Code in the Letter to the Colossians." *Journal for the Study of the New Testament* 79 (2000) 117–30.

Tacitus. *Annals.* 15.44. http://www.perseus.tufts.edu/hopper/text?doc=Perseus%3Atext%3A1999.02.0078%3Abook%3D15%3Achapter%3D44.

Taylor, C. C. W. "Politics." In *The Cambridge Companion to Aristotle*, edited by Jonathan Barnes, 233–58. Cambridge: Cambridge University Press, 1995.

Thurén, Lauri. *The Rhetorical Strategy of 1 Peter, with Special Regard to Ambiguous Expressions.* Turku, Finland: Åbo Academy Press, 1990.

Van Der Horst, Pieter W. "Jewish Funerary Inscriptions—Most are in Greek." *Biblical Archaeology Review* 18 (1992) 46–57.

Vinson, Richard B., et al. *1 & 2 Peter, Jude.* Smyth & Helwys Bible Commentary. Macon, GA: Smyth & Helwys, 2010.

Webb, William J. *Slaves, Women and Homosexuals: Exploring the Hermeneutics of Cultural Analysis.* Downers Grove, IL: IVP Academic, 2001.

Wiedemann, Thomas. *Greek and Roman Slavery.* New York: Routledge, 2005.

Williams, Craig A. *Roman Homosexuality: Ideologies of Masculinity in Classical Antiquity.* Oxford: Oxford University Press, 1999.

Wilson, Woodrow. *A History of the American People: Illustrated With Portraits, Maps, Plans, Facsimiles, Rare Prints, Contemporary Views, Etc.*, vol. 5. New York: Harper & Bros., 1902.

Witherington III, Ben. *Invitation to the New Testament: First Things.* Oxford: Oxford University Press, 2012.

———. *Letters and Homilies for Jewish Christians.* Downers Grove, IL: IVP Academic, 2016.

Zamfir, Korinna. *Men and Women in the Household of God: A Contextual Approach to Roles and Ministries in the Pastoral Epistles.* Göttingen, Germany: Vandenhoeck and Ruprecht, 2013.

Made in the USA
Columbia, SC
28 June 2024

37872072R00085